Game: How to Play the Share Market

Sandeep Chavan

Published by SANDEEP CHAVAN, 2025.

GAME: HOW TO PLAY THE SHARE MARKET

First edition. May 15, 2025.

ISBN: 979-8231704811

Written by Sandeep Chavan.

Table of Contents

Opening Note........1
Preface........3
How to Use This Book........5
Chapter 1: Welcome to the Game........9
Chapter 2: What Even Is the Share Market?........16
Chapter 3: Why Do People Play?........24
Chapter 4: It's Not a Gamble........31
Interlude........39
Chapter 5: Rules of the Game........42
Chapter 6: Every Player Has a Bias........51
Chapter 7: The Playing Field........59
Chapter 8: The Price Is Not the Value........68
Interlude........76
Chapter 9: How to Buy Your First Share........79
Chapter 10: Don't Build a Portfolio........88
Chapter 11: Short-Term Thrills vs. Long-Term Gains........96
Chapter 12: Choosing Companies Like a Player, Not a Fan........104
Chapter 13: Every Move Doesn't Have to Be Brilliant........112
Interlude........120
Chapter 14: Scoreboard Watching Will Kill You........123
Chapter 15: Market Cycles Are Seasons—Not Earthquakes........131
Chapter 16: The Magic Move........139
Chapter 17: When to Sell........146
Chapter 18: Losing Is Also a Move........154
Chapter 19: Your Game Is Not Their Game........161
Interlude........169
Chapter 20: Beyond Stocks........172

Chapter 21: The Future of the Game 180
Chapter 22: Final Word 188
Closing Note 194
Appendix A: Game Glossary 196
Appendix B: Portfolio Blueprint Template 201
Appendix C: Reflective Investor Journal Template 206
Appendix D: Emotional Checklist 211
Appendix E: The 5-Year Letter to My Future Self 215
Investor's Manifesto 220
Further Reading 222
Acknowledgments 226
About the Author 227
Disclaimer 229

To every kind of investor—The cautious beginner, the patient planner,The overthinker, the late starter, the quiet learner,The ones who bought too high, sold too low,And still came back with curiosity.

To the dreamers saving for freedom,The parents investing for their children,The skeptics turned believers,And the believers learning to pause.

Whether you invest in stocks, in funds, in time,Or simply in yourself—

This book is for you. From every corner of the world, with every kind of intent—May you play your game with clarity, calm, and courage.

— *Sandeep*

"The market doesn't reward brilliance.It rewards clarity, patience, and those who can stay calm when others can't."

— *Sandeep Chavan*

Opening Note

This is not a book about the stock market. It's a book about you—finally feeling ready to play.

You don't have to be rich to invest. You don't have to be an expert. You don't need to know what Nifty is. And no, you don't need to follow Elon Musk on Twitter.

You just need to begin.

But most people don't—because the market seems loud, fast, risky, and full of secrets spoken in codes.

They think investing is a battlefield. A roulette table. A genius's playground.

That's the illusion I want to break.

This book is here to tell you: the market is not war. It's not luck. It's not IQ. It's a **game**—and you can learn how to play it, calmly, clearly, and on your own terms.

You won't find hot tips here. You won't learn how to beat algorithms. You won't see charts, buzzwords, or glorified stories of overnight millionaires.

Instead, you'll learn:

- How the share market actually works
- How human emotion moves money more than math
- How to build a portfolio without losing sleep
- And how to grow wealth—not just in numbers, but in mindset

This isn't just a guide. It's a mindset manual. One that helps you invest without noise, chase without panic, and hold without fear.
So if you've ever said:

- "I don't know where to start."
- "I don't want to lose everything."
- "I wish someone just explained it simply..."

This book is for you.
Let's drop the pressure. Let's ignore the noise. And let's finally treat investing for what it really is:
A game. One you're ready to play—without losing your mind.
— *Sandeep*

Preface

Why this book, and why now.

I didn't write this book because I'm a market expert. I wrote it because I've seen too many smart people stay out of the market—not because they lacked money, but because they lacked confidence.

They were afraid of sounding stupid. Afraid of losing everything. Afraid they were too late to begin.

And on the other side, I've seen people jump in with noise, greed, and no plan—treating investing like a lottery with flashing apps and fast exits.

So here we are.

This book is not a get-rich guide. It won't teach you how to beat the system, find hidden gems, or predict the next bull run.

It's about something far more powerful:

How to play the market with patience, purpose, and peace of mind.

I've structured the book into five simple levels:

1. **Understanding the Game** – What this world really is, minus the myths.
2. **Knowing the Rules** – How the market works, and how humans misread it.
3. **Making Your Moves** – What to do (and not do) as you start building.
4. **Staying in the Game** – How to survive, adapt, and

grow during chaos.

5. **Winning Beyond Wealth** – How to define success on your own terms.

Each chapter is short, grounded, and designed for normal life—no jargon, no pressure, no screenshots of stock tips.

Read it straight through, or skip around as needed. Use the appendices as your toolkit. Highlight what resonates. Ignore what doesn't.

But if there's one hope I have, it's this:

That you walk away from this book less afraid, more focused, and fully aware that investing isn't a war—it's a rhythm. One you can learn. One you can trust. One you can play your way.

Welcome to the game.

— *Sandeep*

How to Use This Book

For first-timers, re-starters, and lifelong learners.

This book isn't meant to be read with a calculator in one hand and a stock ticker in the other.

It's meant to be read with a **calm mind.**

Whether you're just starting your investing journey or trying to reset it, this book is here to guide—not overwhelm—you.

Here's how to make the most of it:

Follow the Game Levels (or Don't)

The book is structured like a game—because investing *is* one.

- **Level 1: Understanding the Game** Get grounded. Learn what the market really is—not what the headlines say.
- **Level 2: Knowing the Rules** Explore how the system works—and where most people misplay it.
- **Level 3: Making Your Moves** Start investing. Build a simple, personal strategy that grows with you.
- **Level 4: Staying in the Game** Master resilience, patience, and emotional discipline.
- **Level 5: Winning Beyond Wealth** Redefine success. Build alignment, not just returns.

You can move through the book sequentially, or skip to any level that fits your current stage.

Use the Appendices as Tools

In the back, you'll find a set of actionable, no-fluff tools:

- A Portfolio Blueprint to help you start from zero
- Reflective journal prompts for smarter decision-making
- Emotional checklists to use before buying or selling
- A five-year letter to your future self
- A simple Investor's Manifesto for everyday clarity

Don't rush these. They're not "extras." They're the **practical core**.

Highlight, Scribble, Revisit

You don't need to finish the book in one go. You don't need to remember everything. You only need to take **what clicks with your real life**, and come back later for the rest.
Make notes. Use a sticky tab. Reread a chapter six months from now when the market tests you. That's when the real game begins.

No Prior Knowledge Required

You don't need:

- A finance degree
- A trading account
- A hot stock tip
- A guru whispering in your ear

All you need is **a willingness to think clearly and act calmly**. That's the only entry ticket.

Final Thought

This isn't a book to finish. It's a book to **build with**.
You won't just come out knowing more about the share market. You'll come out knowing more about **how you behave in it—and who you want to be while playing**.
That's how real investors are made.
Let's begin. Turn the page. Level 1 awaits.

LEVEL 1: UNDERSTANDING THE GAME

Chapter 1: Welcome to the Game

But Take Off Your Helmet

Why the market isn't war or roulette. What this book is—and what it isn't.

If you've landed here expecting a cheat code, a hot stock tip, or a fast-track formula to double your money by next month—breathe easy.

You won't find that here. But what you will find is far more valuable: clarity.

Welcome to **Game**—a book about how the share market actually works, how you can be a part of it, and most importantly, how to stay sane while playing.

This isn't a story of overnight millionaires. It's not a motivational chant urging you to "buy the dip" or "never sell." And it's definitely not a crash course in buzzwords, charts, and noise. This is a *thinking person's guide* to a world that's often misunderstood, misused, and misrepresented.

It's time to take off your helmet.

Let's Begin with a Confession

Most people view the share market with equal parts fascination and fear.

They've heard stories of people making fortunes from their smartphones—while sipping coffee. They've also heard of others who lost their life savings, betting on "sure things" that vanished faster than a tweet.

And so, the market becomes this mythical, intimidating beast. A battlefield. A casino. A roller coaster. A place for adrenaline junkies or spreadsheet sorcerers.

But the truth?

The market is neither monster nor magic. It's just a **game**—one that anyone can learn, play, and grow in—if they approach it with strategy, patience, and perspective.

Why "Game"?

We chose the word *game* deliberately. Because that's what this is—a structured, rule-based, interactive, human experience.

In a game:

- There are players.
- There are moves.
- There are wins, losses, and learning.
- And there's always a next turn.

Games reward those who understand the rules, practice consistently, and stay emotionally grounded. They punish the impulsive, the arrogant, and the impatient.

Sound familiar?

The share market isn't about defeating others. It's about defeating your own chaos. The best investors don't "win" in the traditional sense. They *survive, adapt, and evolve.*

This book is here to help you do exactly that.

Why You Don't Need a Helmet

Let's dismantle the most common myth right away:
"The stock market is dangerous."
No. The *lack of understanding* of the stock market is dangerous. Just like a car is not dangerous—until you give it to someone who doesn't know how to drive.
Yes, the market can be volatile. Prices move. Sometimes fast. Sometimes irrationally. But if you approach the market with the right mindset, you don't need protection—you need perspective.
You're not walking into war. You're stepping into a dance of data, emotion, and enterprise. A living organism of belief and behavior.
No helmet required. Just awareness.

What This Book Is

Let's be clear from the start. This book is:

- A rational, grounded guide to understanding the share market
- Written for *ordinary people*, not finance professionals
- Free of heavy jargon, formulas, or trading algorithms
- A mix of philosophy, psychology, and practice
- Designed to help you play long-term—not react short-term

You'll find stories, analogies, practical steps, and mental models to help you *feel at home* in a world often made to feel alien. Whether you're a 22-year-old with your first paycheck, a

40-year-old wondering where your savings went, or a retired school teacher who's always been curious about stocks—this book is for you.

You won't become an expert overnight, but you'll become confident enough to begin playing wisely.

What This Book Isn't

Let's also admit what we won't do.

- We won't predict the next hot stock.
- We won't chase headlines or trends.
- We won't scare you with complex charts.
- And we certainly won't make false promises.

There are enough voices in the world screaming "buy this now!" or "the market is crashing!" This book is the opposite of that. It's quiet. Steady. Focused. It gives you **a long-term lens**—so you can stop reacting and start responding.

Let's Talk About You

You might be thinking:

- "Isn't this just for rich people?"
- "Do I need a finance degree?"
- "Isn't it too risky for someone like me?"
- "Is it too late to start now?"

Here's the truth:

- The market is not just for the wealthy. In fact, many

wealthy people got there *because* they understood how to invest early.

- You don't need a finance degree. You need curiosity, logic, and emotional discipline.
- Risk exists everywhere—crossing the road, starting a business, falling in love. But with education, the share market is one of the *most manageable risks*.
- And no, it's not too late. The market isn't a train you missed. It's a highway you can merge into—at your pace, with your plan.

So whoever you are, however much you've hesitated—consider this your green light.

The Real Game: Not Just Money, But Mind

Here's the real secret no one tells you at the beginning:
The market doesn't test your knowledge. It tests your emotions.
It's not about knowing more. It's about reacting less.
You'll feel excited when your stock rises. You'll feel anxious when it falls. You'll want to chase, flee, double down, or quit.
That's the game.
Not buying. Not selling. The game is your inner response to external noise.
And that's exactly what we'll train in this book.

This Is a Global Game

Markets may be local in flavor—but they're global in nature. Whether you're investing in India, the U.S., Europe, or anywhere else, the fundamentals of smart investing remain the same.

You'll see examples that cross geographies but stay grounded in universal principles. Because ultimately, money behaves like people do—everywhere.

Emotion, trust, fear, greed, and hope are not bound by borders. So if you've ever felt like "the market isn't for people like me," think again.

This is a game *you're already a part of*—whether you play it consciously or not.

How to Read This Book

There's no rush. This isn't a binge-read. It's a conversation. Take your time. Read a chapter, reflect, then read again.

Each chapter stands on its own, but also builds momentum. Think of them as *levels*—not in difficulty, but in depth.

You'll start with what the market is, then move to how it works, how people behave in it, how to participate, and finally—how to stay in the game with grace, patience, and strength.

Read it linearly or skip ahead to what interests you most. But whatever you do—don't treat this like a to-do list. Treat it like a warm-up.

Why This Matters Now, More Than Ever

We live in an era of digital chaos. Information overload. Economic uncertainty. A million voices telling us what to do with our money.

In this noise, two types of people emerge:

- Those who react to every wave, every headline, every whisper.
- And those who learn to play the game with calm clarity.

This book is here to help you become the second kind.
Because if there's one truth we can agree on—it's this:
The future will reward those who can think clearly in a world that panics often.

One Last Thought Before We Begin

The market doesn't need you to be perfect. It doesn't need you to be fearless. It just needs you to show up with a steady mind, a learning spirit, and a long view.
In this game, the biggest edge isn't knowledge. It's behavior.
And the best players? They don't play to beat others. They play to become better versions of themselves—with every move, every mistake, every win.
So, take off the helmet. Grab your curiosity. Let's begin—one move at a time.

Chapter 2: What Even Is the Share Market?

From Wall Street to your phone. The basics, made beautifully simple.

When most people hear the words "share market," the same scene plays out in their heads: A room full of men in suits yelling over blinking screens, colored graphs exploding with data, numbers flying, hands waving like semaphore flags. Somewhere, a TV anchor shouts, "The markets are crashing!" while someone else claims they just doubled their money on a mysterious tech stock.

It feels like chaos. It feels elite. It feels... off-limits.

But here's the first truth no one told you: The market is not a warzone, a casino, or an exclusive club. It's just a system—a tool. And like any tool, it's only as dangerous or powerful as the hands that use it.

So, let's calm the noise. Strip away the drama. And understand what this "share market" really is. You'll see—it's simpler than you think.

Start with the Word "Share"

Let's go back to something you already know.

You order a pizza. Your friends are around. You cut it into eight slices. Everyone takes a piece. Simple sharing.

That's the concept behind a share in business.

A company divides itself into pieces—called shares—and offers them to others. If you buy a share, you now own a tiny part of that business. Its ideas, its buildings, its income, its debts. You're not just betting on it—you're in it.

Now imagine thousands, even millions, of people owning pieces of a company. That's not poetry. That's public ownership. That's exactly what happens when a company "goes public" by listing on the share market.

So, when you hear someone owns 100 shares of a company, remember: they aren't just holding paper or digits on a screen—they own a *fraction of a real business* operating somewhere in the world.

What Is the Share Market, Then?

Picture the world's biggest supermarket of ownership.

Instead of buying groceries, you're buying ownership in businesses. These ownership slices are called *stocks* or *equities*—and the market is the place where they're exchanged.

The share market is simply where people buy and sell belief—in businesses, in economies, in futures.

It doesn't manufacture wealth or magic. It facilitates movement—ownership moving from one person to another, based on how people feel about the future.

This marketplace exists in cities like New York (Wall Street), Mumbai (Dalal Street), London, Tokyo—but also, quietly, invisibly, on the screen in your hand.

From Wall Street to Your Wallet

Once upon a time, investing required brokers, papers, and long phone calls. Today, all you need is a smartphone and an internet connection.

You could be on a beach in Bali, a train in Germany, or a bedroom in Bangalore—you're just a few taps away from buying a piece of the global economy.

Stock exchanges may still sound formal and complex, but they're now digital backbones. Whether it's the NASDAQ, the NSE, or the London Stock Exchange—these platforms act as digital bridges between buyers and sellers, 24/7, around the globe.

And the best part? You don't need a suit, a secretary, or a spreadsheet addiction. You need curiosity, discipline, and clarity.

Why Would a Company Sell Itself in Pieces?

Short answer? To grow.

Imagine you run a thriving bakery. Your products are a hit, customers love you, and you dream of opening ten more branches. But you need more capital to do it.

You have three options:

1. Take a loan from the bank.
2. Find a wealthy investor who'll take a large chunk of your business.
3. Go public—sell shares of your company to everyday people, raise money, and keep building.

In option 3, the bakery becomes a public company. You split it into, say, 100,000 shares. People buy those shares, giving you funds. In return, they become part-owners of your journey.

If the business grows, they win. If it struggles, they share the risk.

That's how the economy works. Businesses raise money. People invest. Everyone is connected through a shared belief in growth.

Two Types of Players: Investors and Traders

Everyone in the share market is playing—but not all are playing the same game.

Investors

They're in it for the long run. They buy shares in companies they believe will grow over time. They think like partners, not customers. They study the business, its management, its vision. They don't care about today's noise—they care about tomorrow's potential.

Think: Warren Buffett, long-term funds, patient capital.

Traders

They're in it for the movement. They buy and sell frequently—sometimes in seconds—based on price swings. They're not building relationships with companies; they're tracking charts, signals, and momentum. It's fast. It's intense. It's not for everyone.

Think: surfing, not swimming.

Both are valid approaches. But this book? It plays the long game. The investor game.
Because while traders chase profits, investors build wealth.

What Moves the Market?

Prices in the market rise and fall constantly. Why?
Because they're driven by perception. Not just hard data. Not just logic. But emotion.
If more people want to buy a stock, its price goes up. If more want to sell it, the price falls. That's basic demand and supply.
But what drives that demand?

- **Company performance** – earnings, losses, new launches
- **Economic signals** – inflation, interest rates, government policy
- **Global news** – elections, wars, pandemics
- **Rumors and sentiment** – media headlines, viral videos
- **Emotion** – fear, greed, hope, hype

The market is a rational system ruled by irrational humans. That's the paradox.

The Two Markets: Primary and Secondary

Let's decode this.

Primary Market

This is where a company sells its shares to the public for the first time. It's called an Initial Public Offering (IPO). Investors buy directly from the company. Like buying a product at launch.

Secondary Market

This is where shares are resold, over and over, between buyers and sellers. You're not buying from the company—you're buying from another investor.
Think: like buying a used car. The car doesn't change—only the owner does.
This is the part we usually call "the stock market."

How Do You Actually Buy a Share?

Here's the typical journey:

1. **Choose a platform or broker** – Zerodha, Robinhood, Fidelity, etc.
2. **Open your trading + demat account** – one to buy, the other to hold.
3. **Transfer funds** from your bank.
4. **Search for the stock** you're interested in.
5. **Click "Buy."**
6. **Done**—you now own a piece of a company.

No ceremonies. No VIP entry. Just clarity and a couple of clicks.

Why Do Prices Change Every Second?

Because people change their minds every second.
New headlines, a viral tweet, a policy speech, a bad earnings report—anything can shift sentiment. And when perception shifts, prices follow.
Markets are dynamic because people are dynamic. They reflect everything we think, feel, and fear—in real time.

Is This All Just Fancy Gambling?

It depends on how you play.
If you throw money blindly, chase tips, and react to every price movement—then yes, it's speculation. But if you study, observe, and invest with purpose—then it's strategy.
The market gives you the same set of tools. It's your behavior that determines whether you're investing or just gambling in a suit.

What Do You Actually Get When You Buy a Share?

You don't just get a digital receipt. You get:

- Voting rights (in many cases)
- A slice of profits (via dividends, if declared)
- Capital appreciation (if the stock rises in value)
- Transparency (access to company reports and data)
- A relationship with risk (your shares can fall in value)

But importantly—you only lose what you invest. You're not liable for company debts. You're a shareholder, not a guarantor.

So Why Should You Even Care?

Because investing isn't just about money.
It's about:

- Ownership in the world's most powerful businesses
- Wealth-building through discipline, not luck
- Compounding, where small grows into mighty
- Choice, in where your money aligns with your beliefs

Buying a stock isn't shouting into the wind. It's a quiet declaration: "I believe in this idea. I'm part of it."

Final Analogy: The Farmer and the Field

Think of your money as seeds. The share market is the field. Each company is a different crop. Your understanding? That's the weather.
Scatter seeds randomly—and you might get lucky. Plant them thoughtfully, water them, wait with patience—and you get a harvest.
That's what investing is.

One-Line Summary

The share market is where belief meets business, logic meets emotion, and value is exchanged—not just in dollars, but in decisions.

Chapter 3: Why Do People Play?

The motivations behind investing—freedom, wealth, curiosity, or pressure?

Before we dive into strategies, charts, and choices, let's take a pause.

Let's ask a simple but powerful question: Why are you here?

Why are you reading a book about the share market? Why does investing suddenly seem important, interesting, or even urgent?

What made you stop and think: "Maybe I should play this game"?

That "why" matters more than you think.

Because in the long run, your *motivation* will influence your *decisions*. And your decisions will determine whether you panic, persist, or prosper.

So in this chapter, we'll explore the most common reasons people join the market—and how understanding your reason is the first step toward playing well.

1. The Pursuit of Wealth: "I want to grow my money."

This is the most obvious and most popular answer:

"I want to invest so I can build wealth."

And that's completely valid.

The share market is one of the few tools in the world that allows *anyone*, from *anywhere*, with *any background*, to participate in economic growth.

You don't need a business empire. You don't need millions in savings. You don't even need to "know someone."

You can start with a few dollars—or rupees—and scale up. Over time, as businesses grow, economies expand, and innovation accelerates, your money gets to *ride the wave*.

That's the essence of long-term investing.

You're not chasing money. You're partnering with value.

Investing isn't about becoming rich overnight. It's about becoming independent over time.

But here's a small warning: if your only motivation is money—and that too *fast money*—you'll be tempted to jump into risky bets, chase hype, or quit too soon when things wobble.

So if wealth is your reason, make sure it's sustainable wealth, not sudden excitement.

2. The Search for Freedom: "I don't want to depend on anyone."

There's another, deeper reason many people come to the market—one they don't always say out loud.

It's the desire for freedom.

Not the Instagram version with palm trees and laptops on beaches. But real freedom: to make choices without fear. To walk away from a toxic job. To retire early and live on your own terms. To support your family without constantly counting every expense. To breathe easier.

The market, when approached patiently, can help you build that kind of freedom.

It doesn't guarantee it. But it offers the path.

That path is built on discipline, delayed gratification, and long-term consistency—not adrenaline.

If this is your motivation, good. It's one of the strongest ones. Just remember: freedom doesn't come from chasing gains. It comes from building habits that align with your values and give you control over time.

In this game, your money grows as you grow. And freedom? That's the real compounding.

3. The Spark of Curiosity: "How does this thing work?"

Some people are just curious. And curiosity is powerful.

They hear about IPOs. They see finance influencers. They catch bits of news about the S&P 500 or the Nifty. And a part of their brain lights up with the question: "What is this world? How does it work?"

They don't enter for money or status. They enter for understanding.

They want to decode the system. See behind the curtain. And somewhere along the way, they begin to appreciate how markets are living systems—where psychology, politics, economics, technology, and human behavior all collide.

If that's you—welcome. Your mindset is wired for long-term learning.

Curiosity-based investors often end up making better decisions. Why? Because they seek *clarity*, not *certainty*.

They ask better questions. They don't chase trends blindly. They watch, observe, learn, and slowly build conviction.

If you stay curious, the market becomes a school—not a trap.

4. The Pressure Cooker: "Everyone else is investing—I should too."

This one's a bit uncomfortable, but important.

A lot of people start investing because of peer pressure.

They see friends making "quick money" on crypto. Or someone at work won't shut up about that one stock they picked. Or influencers on social media flash their "portfolio screenshots" like they're lottery tickets.

Suddenly, you feel left behind. You feel guilty. "Am I missing something?" "Why am I not in the game?" "I should do *something* before it's too late!"

This is called FOMO—Fear Of Missing Out. And it's one of the worst reasons to start investing.

Not because investing is wrong. But because you're starting from emotion, not intention.

When the market goes up, you feel smart. When it drops, you feel stupid—and you blame the market.

This emotional rollercoaster is not sustainable.

So if pressure is your entry point, that's okay. We all start somewhere. But let's evolve from that. Let's pause and ask:

"Am I investing because I believe in this—or because I don't want to feel left out?"

5. The Legacy Builder: "I want to leave something behind."

For some, the market isn't about themselves. It's about their *next generation*.

They want to build assets that outlive them. Support their children's education. Gift their grandchildren a portfolio instead of a photo album.

They see investing not as a game of returns, but as an act of responsibility.

If that's your reason, beautiful. That kind of thinking brings focus, patience, and humility.

Long-term investing is, in many ways, an act of love across time. You're planting trees whose shade you may never sit under—but someone else will.

6. The Quiet Rebel: "I want control over my own destiny."

Some people play this game because they're tired of dependency. Tired of financial systems that don't serve them. Tired of waiting for governments, jobs, or bosses to create safety.

They turn to the market as a way to take back control.

They may start small, but they grow with purpose. They learn not because they're forced to, but because they *want* to. They reject blind obedience and instead seek personal agency.

If that resonates with you—you're not alone.

Millions of independent thinkers have turned to the market as a quiet revolution. Not to become millionaires—but to stop feeling powerless.

Investing is not just economic. For many, it's deeply personal.

Understanding Your Own Why

Let's pause. Which of these reasons speaks to you?

- Wealth?
- Freedom?
- Curiosity?
- Pressure?
- Legacy?
- Rebellion?

Maybe it's a mix of two or three. Maybe it's changed over time. Whatever it is, write it down. Be honest. Because your "why" will shape your "how."

If your motivation is clear, your strategy becomes easier. If your motivation is confused, your decisions become scattered.

Let's Play an Example Out

Two people start investing.

Aman is doing it because everyone at his office is into stocks. He doesn't want to look like the only one who isn't "financially smart." He buys hot stocks without research, panics during drops, and sells at a loss.

Reena, on the other hand, wants long-term independence. She starts small, reads one article a week, ignores noise, and adds money monthly to 3 companies she understands.

Guess who survives the market long enough to win?

The one who plays from within—not from fear.

Your "Why" Can Evolve

Maybe you started because of pressure. That's okay. Maybe you now feel curious. That's great. Maybe one day it becomes about building legacy. Beautiful.

Your "why" is allowed to change—just like you do. The key is to check in with yourself once in a while and ask:

"Am I still playing the game *I* chose? Or did I get pulled into someone else's?"

That self-awareness is the most underrated skill in investing.

Final Thought: The Market Is a Mirror

Ultimately, the share market is not just a collection of numbers. It's a mirror. It reflects not just economies—but *you*.

Your mindset. Your emotions. Your beliefs about risk, reward, success, and security.

So before you place your first trade or build your portfolio, look inward.

Ask not:

"What should I buy?"

Ask:

"Why am I even playing?"

One-Line Summary

In the game of investing, knowing your *why* is your first real move—and your most honest advantage.

Chapter 4: It's Not a Gamble

Unless You Treat It Like One

What separates mindful investing from blind speculation.

Let's get straight to the point: The most common accusation thrown at the share market is this:

"It's just gambling in a suit."

To someone unfamiliar with how investing actually works, it *can* look like gambling. Prices go up, prices go down. People win, people lose. There's risk. There's excitement. There are even phrases that sound like poker slang—"double down," "all in," "betting on a turnaround."

So the skepticism is understandable.

But here's the catch: the market isn't gambling. It only becomes gambling when you treat it like a game of chance, not a system of decisions.

The difference lies not in the stock—but in you.

Let's unpack that.

The Core Difference: Chance vs. Choice

Gambling is rooted in *chance*. The outcome is random. You pull a lever, roll a dice, or flip a card. No matter how confident you are, you cannot control the outcome. Skill may help in managing your bets, but the core event is probabilistic and unpredictable.

Investing, on the other hand, is rooted in *choice*. You study a business, its leadership, its industry, its potential. You assess whether the price makes sense for what you're getting. You aren't trying to guess a number. You're making a decision based on information.

Gambling is guessing. Investing is reasoning.

You can't predict the future with certainty in either case—but in investing, you stack the odds by using your mind. You play with intention, not instinct.

So Why Do People Confuse the Two?

Let's be honest: many people enter the market with the wrong expectations.

They see:

- Overnight "multibaggers" promoted on social media
- Crypto success stories (minus the crash posts)
- Friends who made "easy" money in the last bull run
- TV anchors hyping stocks like racehorses

In such an environment, it's no surprise that the share market feels like Vegas wearing a tie.

The line between speculation and investment starts to blur when people:

- Buy without understanding the business
- Follow trends without conviction
- Panic at every price drop
- Obsess over short-term gains
- Chase tips instead of building a process

If you're just throwing money at something because someone said it'll rise—yes, you're gambling.
But if you're thoughtfully choosing businesses and giving them time to grow—you're investing.
The *market stays the same*. The *mindset defines the method.*

Mindful Investing: What It Looks Like

Let's define what mindful investing actually means.
Mindful investing is:

- Intentional – You know *why* you're investing.
- Informed – You understand what you're buying and why it has value.
- Patient – You give time for your thesis to play out.
- Calm – You don't react impulsively to market noise.
- Aligned – Your investments match your goals and risk comfort.

You're not trying to impress anyone. You're not trying to get rich in 90 days. You're building long-term value—step by step, stock by stock.
Think of it as planting trees, not spinning wheels.
The results don't show immediately. But over years, the forest grows.

Speculation: When You Cross the Line

Now let's look at speculative behavior—when investing loses its soul and becomes thrill-seeking.
Speculation is when:

- You buy a stock only because it's trending
- You don't even know what the company does
- You check prices every hour
- You invest more after seeing green candles on charts—not business results
- You panic-sell at the first sign of red
- You treat every rumor like gospel truth

This behavior mimics gambling—because it's reactive, emotional, and disconnected from reality.
Ironically, many people who call the market a gamble are unknowingly approaching it like gamblers themselves.

Risk Isn't the Enemy—It's the Price of Entry

Here's the uncomfortable truth:
There is no such thing as a risk-free investment.
Even your savings in a bank lose value to inflation over time.
Risk is not evil. It's energy. It's the *uncertainty that allows for possibility.*
Without risk, there is no reward. But not all risks are equal.
The key is to understand the risk you're taking—not to eliminate it.
Let's break it down:

Type of Risk	Investing	Gambling
Nature	Strategic	Random
Outcome control	Partial (via research & discipline)	None
Time horizon	Long-term	Immediate
Value basis	Business fundamentals	Luck/probability
Learning curve	Steep but cumulative	Repetitive and chance-based

So when someone says, "Isn't the stock market risky?"—the answer is *yes, but so is life*. The goal isn't to avoid risk. The goal is to manage it mindfully.

An Analogy You'll Remember: Chess vs. Dice

Think of investing like playing chess, not rolling dice.

In chess, you don't know what your opponent will do—but you plan, you adapt, you think ahead. You don't control the whole game, but your choices matter deeply.

In dice, you just roll and hope.

Now, here's the twist: the market has *elements* of both. You can never predict it fully. But over time, the player who thinks, studies, and plays with discipline wins more than they lose.

If you treat the market like dice, you'll chase thrill. If you treat it like chess, you'll build mastery.

The Role of Luck: Yes, It Exists—But It's Not a Strategy

People get lucky in the market. Just like someone might win their first poker hand or first coin toss.

But if your plan is built on *luck*, you don't have a plan. You have a fantasy.

Good investing acknowledges luck—but relies on process.

The most successful investors in the world will tell you:

- "I don't aim to be right all the time. I aim to survive long enough to benefit when I *am* right."
- "I protect my downside first, then let the upside take care of itself."
- "I don't invest based on noise. I invest based on clarity."

These are not gamblers. These are strategic players.

What Happens When You Treat It Like a Gamble

Let's talk consequences.

When you gamble in the market:

- You get addicted to thrill. You check prices every minute. You confuse movement with progress.
- You ignore fundamentals. You care more about charts and trends than business logic.
- You chase losses. After a fall, you double down emotionally—hoping to recover fast.
- You burn out. Emotionally, financially, mentally.

The market will not adapt to your mood. It will continue doing what it does—testing your discipline every step of the way.

And if you're playing with emotion, not strategy, you'll eventually run out of patience—or money.

Reframing Risk: Educated Risk Is a Skill

You can't remove risk from the game. But you can change your relationship with it.
Here's how:

1. Understand what you're investing in. If you can't explain a company's business to a 10-year-old, you probably shouldn't invest in it.
2. Size your bets wisely. Don't put half your savings in one hot stock. Allocate with balance.
3. Diversify. Spread across sectors and geographies. One bad bet shouldn't ruin the game.
4. Have a timeframe. Know whether this is a 5-month trade or a 5-year investment.
5. Accept volatility. Price swings are part of the journey. Don't confuse noise with signal.

Investing isn't about avoiding pain. It's about understanding it—*and preparing for it*.

Your Mind Is the Real Battleground

Ultimately, the difference between gambling and investing lies in one place: your head.
Two people can buy the same stock at the same time. One is gambling. The other is investing.
Same action. Different intention. Different outcome.
The market is neutral. You are not.

So train your mind. Build your framework. And approach the market like a calm player, not a desperate spinner of wheels.

Final Example: Riya and Kartik

Riya starts investing with a plan. She picks five companies she understands, spreads her capital over time, reviews once a quarter, and avoids reacting to headlines.

Kartik jumps into every "hot" stock his friends talk about, buys high, panics when it drops, and keeps refreshing his portfolio every hour.

Two people. Same market. One is building wealth. The other is just... *playing with fire.*

Which one are you becoming?

One-Line Summary

The market becomes a gamble only when you stop thinking and start reacting—investing is the art of making calm choices in a noisy world.

Interlude

Before You Make Your First Move

So far, you haven't picked a stock. You haven't opened an account. You haven't placed a trade.

But you've already done something far more important: You've understood what this game really is.

That's where most people go wrong. They start without clarity. They play without perspective. They confuse luck with logic, movement with mastery, price with value.

But you? You now know better.

You've realized:

- The share market is not a battlefield or casino—it's a marketplace of belief.
- A "share" isn't a magic code—it's part ownership in a real business.
- The motivations behind investing aren't all financial—they're deeply personal.
- Risk is not the villain—mindless behavior is.
- And finally: this game is not about beating others—it's about not losing to yourself.

You've crossed the noise. You've found your footing. You're not here to chase hype. You're here to play with purpose.

That matters.

Because in the world of investing, understanding the game before you play is your first real edge.

The next level will move from philosophy to mechanics. We'll talk rules. Structure. Boundaries. Mistakes to avoid. Tools to use.

But never forget: Mindset is your first asset.

And now that yours is aligned—Let's step forward with focus.

Level 2: Knowing The Rules

Chapter 5: Rules of the Game

What You Must Understand Before You Start

Market basics, timeframes, risk, rewards—and your own mindset.

You wouldn't walk into a chess tournament without knowing how the pieces move. You wouldn't jump into a soccer match without learning the offside rule. And you definitely wouldn't fly a plane by just "feeling it out."

So why do so many people start investing without understanding the rules of the game?

Here's the truth: You don't need to be a genius to invest well. But you do need to respect the structure.

That's what this chapter is about—not hype, not hot tips, but the basic rules you need to understand before placing your first order.

These are your *guardrails*, your *checkpoints*, your *mental map*.

They won't tell you which stock to buy. But they'll help you play like someone who intends to stay in the game, not just crash in the first round.

Rule 1: The Market Is a System—Not a Mystery

At first glance, the market feels wild. Prices flicker. News hits. People panic. It seems unpredictable—like a crowd without a leader.

But underneath all that chaos is a system. A structure. A set of rules.

- Companies list their shares.
- Investors and traders buy and sell them.
- Exchanges provide the platform.
- Prices move based on supply, demand, and perception.
- Data flows constantly—quarterly results, global events, political changes.

It's not magic. It's not mood. It's *mechanics.*
When you begin to see the structure, the noise fades. You stop treating the market like a mood ring and start treating it like a living organism—with habits, triggers, and seasons.
You don't have to master it all. But you do need to respect its logic.

Rule 2: Your Timeframe Shapes Your Game

This one's non-negotiable.
Before you click "Buy," ask yourself:
"How long am I willing to stay invested in this?"
Because time isn't just a background detail in investing—it's the whole landscape.
There are three broad timeframes to understand:
1. Short-Term (Days to Months)

- You're reacting to news, momentum, earnings announcements.
- This is usually where traders operate.

- It's fast, emotional, and needs constant attention.
- Risk of loss: High
- Risk of burnout: Even higher

2. Medium-Term (1–3 Years)

- You're betting on recovery or transformation.
- You're still checking regularly, but not daily.
- Risk is manageable if you've chosen wisely.

3. Long-Term (5+ Years)

- You're betting on the business, not the moment.
- You care about cash flow, leadership, market position.
- You let compounding do the heavy lifting.
- You sleep better.

The market rewards patience—not perfection.
Choosing your timeframe sets the tone for everything else: What you buy, how you evaluate it, when you exit, and how you handle volatility.
Your job isn't to find the "best" timeframe. Your job is to find your timeframe.

Rule 3: Prices Fluctuate—That's Not the Same as Losing Money

Let's clear up a common fear: You bought a stock for $50. The next day, it's at $46. Did you "lose" $4?
Technically, yes. Realistically? Not unless you sell.

Price drops are part of the game. They're not failures—they're fluctuations.
In fact, if your investment never fluctuates, it's probably not growing either.
Markets go through:

- **Daily noise** – random ups and downs with no long-term meaning
- **Short-term dips** – triggered by news, sentiment, or rumors
- **Corrections** – 10–20% drops that happen even in healthy markets
- **Crashes** – sharp declines due to fear, crises, or global shifts

A fall in price is not a signal to flee. It's a signal to reflect.
Ask:

- "Has the company changed?"
- "Has my reason for investing changed?"
- "Is this emotion or logic speaking?"

If nothing's changed except the screen turning red, maybe the best move is to sit still.

Rule 4: Risk and Reward Are Married—You Can't Separate Them

There is no "high reward, zero risk" scenario. That's not investing—that's a scam.
Every investment comes with a trade-off:

- High risk → potential for high reward, but more volatility
- Low risk → more stability, but slower growth

Your job is not to avoid risk. Your job is to:

- Understand it
- Accept it
- Plan for it

Ask yourself:

- "Can I afford to lose this money?"
- "Will I panic if it drops by 20%?"
- "Am I betting or building?"

A common mistake? Investing money you need soon in high-risk stocks. That's not brave—it's reckless.
The moment your risk exceeds your emotional capacity, the game turns against you.

Rule 5: Your Mindset Is More Important Than Your Math

You can know all the formulas. You can read the news. You can track every technical indicator.
But if you can't handle your own psychology, the market will chew you up.
Because here's what really happens:

- Stocks drop. Your brain screams, "Sell!"
- Stocks rise. Your brain whispers, "Buy more. Don't

miss out."
- Everyone's talking about a stock. You feel FOMO.
- A rumor hits. You panic, even if it's false.

This is not a numbers game. It's a nerves game.
Your emotions are your real opponents.
Winning in the market is often not about outsmarting others.
It's about not outsmarting yourself into mistakes.
So build a mindset that's:

- Calm under pressure
- Curious, not impulsive
- More focused on *process* than *prediction*
- Willing to be wrong—but quick to learn

Rule 6: You Don't Need to Know Everything—But You Need to Know Enough

Let's remove the pressure right now: You don't need to become a financial analyst. You don't need to memorize ratios. You don't need to understand the Greek alphabet of investing.
But you do need to understand what you're buying.
Before you invest, ask:

- "What does this company actually do?"
- "How does it make money?"
- "Why do I think it will grow?"
- "Who's running it?"
- "What am I paying for it?"

If you can't answer these in simple terms, you're guessing—not investing.
Simplicity is not stupidity. It's strength.
If you can't explain your investment to a friend without using jargon—you probably don't understand it yet.

Rule 7: Nothing Works Instantly—But Everything Compounds Eventually

This rule is quiet—but it's the most powerful of them all.
The market rewards:

- Time in the market—not timing the market
- Consistent action—not dramatic moves
- Boring discipline—not loud predictions

You won't feel smart in your first month. You might even feel lost.
But if you keep learning, keep showing up, and avoid the urge to gamble—you'll start to see something magical: Compounding.
It starts slow. Invisible, almost. Then one day, your portfolio looks back at you and says, "See? I was growing all along."

Rule 8: You Must Build a System—Not Follow Moods

Lastly, this game isn't played with vibes and guesses. It's played with systems.
Your system could be simple:

- "I invest 10% of my income every month."

- "I pick companies I understand and hold them for 5 years."
- "I don't react to headlines unless it affects fundamentals."
- "I check my portfolio only once a month."

Whatever it is, have one. Because in moments of panic, your system saves you. In moments of greed, your system grounds you.

A good system is like a seatbelt. You may not notice it—but you'll be glad it's there when things shake.

Checklist: Are You Ready to Start?

Before you buy your first share, run this quick internal test:

- ☐ Do I know my goal? (Wealth, freedom, legacy, etc.)
- ☐ Do I know my timeframe? (Months vs. years)
- ☐ Do I know my risk appetite? (Low, medium, high)
- ☐ Am I investing money I don't need immediately?
- ☐ Do I understand what I'm buying?
- ☐ Do I have a plan for market dips?
- ☐ Am I willing to be patient—even if nothing happens for months?

If you checked most of these—you're ready. Not to "win the market." But to play it wisely.

One-Line Summary

Before you enter the market, learn its rhythm, set your pace, and align your expectations—because how you begin often shapes how you endure.

Chapter 6: Every Player Has a Bias

Behavioral traps: fear, greed, ego, herd thinking, FOMO.

The share market is not just a place where businesses get valued and prices move. It's a playground for the human mind—yours included.

If investing were purely logical, we'd all be rich. But it's not. Because the mind is not a spreadsheet. It's a swirling ocean of memories, stories, emotions, and impulses.

Every investor brings their beliefs, fears, ambitions, and scars to the table. Some know it. Most don't.

That's why this chapter exists.

Because before you conquer the market, you need to confront your own bias.

What Is a Bias, Anyway?

A bias is a mental shortcut. A default reaction. A way your brain tries to simplify reality based on past experience, instinct, or social influence.

Bias isn't inherently bad. It helps us navigate a complex world quickly. But in investing, bias distorts perception. It makes you think you're making rational choices—when you're actually reacting emotionally or socially.

Bias is the silent saboteur of intelligent investing.

It doesn't shout. It whispers. It doesn't fight. It persuades. And the worst part? You often don't even know it's happening.

Let's unmask the main culprits.

1. Fear – The Paralysis Bias

Fear shows up like this:

- "What if the market crashes after I buy?"
- "What if I lose my savings?"
- "What if I'm wrong?"
- "What if this isn't the right time?"

Fear keeps you stuck on the sidelines, overanalyzing, waiting for "the perfect moment" that never comes.
The problem?

- Fear convinces you that inaction is safe. But doing nothing is also a choice—with consequences.
- It makes you focus on worst-case scenarios while ignoring long-term potential.
- It frames every dip as a disaster, not a discount.

Fear makes you freeze when you should stay steady.
How to counter it:

- Accept that no investment is risk-free.
- Start small to build comfort.
- Remember: time reduces risk—but fear amplifies it.
- Reframe dips as *volatility*, not *failure*.

2. Greed – The Overreach Bias

Greed whispers:

- "This stock has doubled—I should put in more."

- "Why settle for 12% returns when crypto is doing 50%?"
- "If I just take a little more risk, I could retire early."
- "Everyone else is getting rich. Why not me?"

Greed makes you overweight bad bets, ignore warning signs, and chase unsustainable growth.

And ironically, it feels smart while you're doing it. Greed wears the costume of ambition—but it plays the game of *impatience.*

Greed doesn't just make you reach. It makes you *overreach*—right before the fall.

How to counter it:

- Set target returns based on reality, not social media.
- Diversify—don't go "all in" on any one idea.
- Celebrate gains with caution, not euphoria.
- Always ask: "Am I investing—or am I hoping?"

3. Ego – The Confirmation Bias

Ego bias makes you believe you're right—and seek evidence that proves it.

You buy a stock, and now every article you read just "happens" to confirm your choice. You ignore bad news, downplay risks, and avoid listening to dissenting views.

This is called confirmation bias, and it's deadly.

Ego bias also manifests in these thoughts:

- "I can't be wrong. I did my research."
- "They just don't understand the stock like I do."
- "This loss is temporary—it'll bounce back because I

said so."

Here, you stop evaluating and start defending. The stock becomes an extension of your identity. And that's where danger begins.

The moment you think you're immune to mistakes, you're already making one.

How to counter it:

- Write down *why* you're investing before you buy. Review it later with honesty.
- Follow people who challenge your views, not just validate them.
- Accept that being wrong is part of the game—and survival is more important than pride.
- Separate your *ego* from your *equity*.

4. Herd Thinking – The Crowd Bias

Ever felt this?

- "Everyone's buying it—maybe I should too."
- "If so many people are excited, it must be good."
- "I don't want to miss out on the next big thing."

That's herd bias—when we copy others because it feels safer than thinking independently.

It's ancient biology. In the wild, staying with the group increased chances of survival. But in the market, following the herd can lead you straight off a cliff.

Because crowds don't analyze. Crowds react. Crowds move fast—but not always forward.
The herd feels comforting—until it runs in the wrong direction.
How to counter it:

- Ask: "Would I still buy this stock if no one else was talking about it?"
- Slow down during hype cycles.
- Zoom out and check if the business actually matches the buzz.
- Remember: if you follow the herd during the boom, you may follow them into the bust.

5. FOMO – The Regret Bias

Fear of Missing Out may be the most dangerous emotion in modern investing.
It triggers when:

- A friend posts their "crazy returns."
- A YouTuber screams "10X potential!"
- A stock jumps 25% in a week and you weren't in it.
- The media says, "If you didn't buy this stock, you missed the train."

FOMO makes you invest out of panic, not logic. You chase rallies. You buy too late. You enter trends without understanding. And when things go south, regret hits twice as hard—because deep down, you knew you didn't think it through.

FOMO turns investors into passengers—people who jump onto moving vehicles without checking the destination.
How to counter it:

- Have a strategy. FOMO thrives in the absence of one.
- Ask yourself: "Is this urgency, or is this understanding?"
- Accept that you will miss some opportunities—and that's okay.
- Focus on playing *your* game—not someone else's highlight reel.

Why Knowing These Biases Matters

You don't remove bias by reading about it. But you *weaken its grip* by becoming aware of it.
Once you start noticing your triggers—fear, hype, ego, social pressure—you regain control.
You stop reacting. You start *responding*.
Most people lose money in the market not because of bad stocks—but because of bad timing caused by unchecked emotions.
The moment you confuse *how you feel* with *what's true*, bias wins.

The Investor's Mind: Calm, Curious, and Self-Aware

Let's redefine what makes a good investor—not in terms of returns, but resilience.
A great investor is:

- Calm in the face of volatility
- Patient in the face of noise
- Curious in the face of uncertainty
- Disciplined in the face of temptation
- Detached in the face of loss

This doesn't mean you become a robot. It means you become a reflective human.

You pause before pressing "buy." You think before following trends. You invest because you believe—not because you're bored.

That's how real players win—not in every trade, but across time.

A Simple Daily Practice: The Bias Check-In

Before you make a market decision, ask:

- "Am I afraid?"
- "Am I greedy?"
- "Am I trying to prove I'm right?"
- "Am I following the crowd?"
- "Am I chasing something just because others are?"

If you answer "yes" to any of these—pause. Step back. Recheck your reasoning.

Because the most powerful move in investing is not always buying or selling. Sometimes, it's waiting.

Final Thought: The Market Tests Your Mind More Than Your Money

It's easy to open an account. Easy to click "buy." Easy to follow a tip. Harder to stay grounded.

This chapter wasn't about technical analysis or financial ratios. It was about *psychological hygiene.*

Because in the end, your brain is your brokerage.

If you don't master your mind, the market will do it for you—and not kindly.

One-Line Summary

Every investor has a bias—but the ones who win are the ones who see it, name it, and rise above it.

Chapter 7: The Playing Field

Exchanges, Indices, and Institutions

What the market is made of—from companies to platforms.

Imagine trying to play a game without knowing the field.

You've got the players. You've read the rules. You're ready to make your move. But—wait. Where is this happening? What's the court? The arena? The platform?

In investing, that's what this chapter is all about: Understanding the actual playing field—the exchanges, the indices, and the institutions that make up the environment where all this action unfolds.

Because if you don't understand the arena, you'll always feel like a visitor—not a player.

1. Stock Exchanges: Where the Game Is Played

Let's start with the most basic—and most important—venue in the share market: the stock exchange.

A stock exchange is like a marketplace. But instead of buying apples or electronics, people buy and sell ownership in companies—in the form of *shares*.

Major Exchanges Around the World

Some of the most prominent stock exchanges include:

- *New York Stock Exchange (NYSE) – USA*

- *NASDAQ – USA (tech-heavy)*
- *London Stock Exchange (LSE) – UK*
- *Tokyo Stock Exchange (TSE) – Japan*
- *Shanghai Stock Exchange – China*
- *National Stock Exchange (NSE) – India*
- *Bombay Stock Exchange (BSE) – India*
- *Deutsche Börse (Xetra) – Germany*

Each exchange acts like a digital arena. Companies list their shares there, and investors across the world place orders via brokers connected to those exchanges.
If a company is the "player," the exchange is the "stadium" where its value is constantly being scored and updated.

How It Works

- Every share has a bid price (what buyers are willing to pay) and an ask price (what sellers are asking for).
- The exchange matches these bids and asks in real time.
- This creates the current market price you see when you look up a stock.

It happens millions of times a day. Quietly. Rapidly. And now, thanks to online platforms—you can participate from anywhere.

2. Stock Indices: The Scoreboards of the Market

Now imagine trying to understand how a football league is doing—but you're only watching one player.
That's where indices come in.

A stock index is a collection of companies—usually the biggest or most representative ones—that give you a snapshot of the market's mood and movement.

It's like a scoreboard. It tells you whether the game is going up, down, or sideways—without showing every single move by every single player.

Famous Indices

- **S&P 500** – 500 large US companies; a key benchmark of the US economy.
- **Dow Jones Industrial Average (DJIA)** – 30 major US companies.
- **NASDAQ Composite** – Primarily tech companies in the US.
- **FTSE 100** – Top 100 companies on the London Stock Exchange.
- **Nikkei 225** – Japan's leading index.
- **Sensex** – Top 30 companies on BSE (India).
- **Nifty 50** – Top 50 companies on NSE (India).

These indices don't include all stocks. They're selective—but they reflect the market's pulse.

When the media says "The market is up today," they're usually referring to an index.

Think of indices as the temperature reading of an entire economy.

A single stock may be cold or hot—but the index shows the weather across the field.

3. The Role of Institutions: The Big Players on the Field

Now let's talk about the giants on the field—the institutional investors.

These aren't individuals buying 10 or 100 shares. These are massive organizations controlling billions or trillions in capital. They include:

- **Mutual Funds** – Collect money from many people and invest on their behalf.
- **Pension Funds** – Manage retirement savings for millions of workers.
- **Insurance Companies** – Invest premiums collected from policyholders.
- **Sovereign Wealth Funds** – Government-run investment funds.
- **Hedge Funds** – Specialized funds that take high-risk, high-return positions.
- **Exchange-Traded Funds (ETFs)** – Funds that track indices and trade like stocks.

These players don't just participate in the market—they influence it. When they buy or sell large quantities of shares, prices shift.

They often have teams of analysts, algorithms, and insider-level insights. But they also face limitations—like regulatory scrutiny, limited flexibility, and pressure to outperform.

Why Institutions Matter to You

Even if you're a small investor, institutions affect you:

- They move markets when they enter or exit a stock.
- Their long-term confidence can stabilize a company's stock price.
- Their portfolio reports can be studied for inspiration.

But don't blindly copy them. Their scale and strategies are different. They may buy a stock *you* shouldn't—because their risk tolerance and objectives are far more complex.
Remember: Just because a whale swims in a direction doesn't mean the fish should follow.

4. Market Participants: Who Else Is Playing?

Besides institutions and companies, here's who you share the field with:

Retail Investors (People like you and me)

The fastest-growing force. Millions of individual investors using apps to invest with as little as $10 or ₹100.
Retail investors are:

- Agile, because they can make decisions quickly.
- Vulnerable, because they often react emotionally or follow the crowd.
- Powerful, when acting collectively—as we saw in the GameStop saga.

Brokerage Platforms

You can't access the exchange directly. You need a broker—a licensed intermediary that connects your order to the market. Brokers may be:

- Full-service (offering research, advisory, and portfolio support)
- Discount or online-only (cheap, efficient, self-service)

Examples:

- Robinhood, Charles Schwab, Fidelity (US)
- Zerodha, Upstox, Groww (India)
- Saxo, eToro, Interactive Brokers (Global)

The broker provides:

- Trading interface
- Account management
- Real-time quotes
- Historical data
- Research tools

Choose one that suits your style and comfort—not just lowest cost.

5. The Regulatory Backbone: Keeping the Game Clean

No field is safe without a referee. In the market, those referees are the regulators.

These bodies ensure:

- Companies don't lie to investors
- Market manipulation is prevented
- Retail investors aren't misled
- Insider trading is punished
- Transparency is enforced

Key Regulators Around the World

- SEBI – Securities and Exchange Board of India
- SEC – Securities and Exchange Commission (USA)
- FCA – Financial Conduct Authority (UK)
- ESMA – European Securities and Markets Authority
- ASIC – Australian Securities and Investments Commission

These institutions don't guarantee zero risk—but they try to ensure fair play.
Investing is a game of risk—but it shouldn't be a game of deception.

How to Navigate the Field as a Thoughtful Player

So now that you understand the layout, how do you play it smart?

Use indices to observe, not to obsess.

Track Nifty or S&P 500 to sense trends—but don't treat them like gospel. You don't have to mimic the index. Sometimes, the best opportunities lie outside the spotlight.

Respect institutions—but play your own game.

You're not managing a billion-dollar portfolio. You don't need to "beat" anyone. Focus on clarity, not comparison.

Choose a broker that aligns with your comfort.

Don't overpay for features you don't use. But don't go so cheap that you compromise support or security.

Know the rules—but focus on* how *you play.

Everyone plays on the same field. What separates winners is not access—but approach.

Final Reflection: The Market Is Not Just a Place—It's an Ecosystem

It's easy to think of the stock market as just "some app where prices go up or down." But now you know—it's far more layered.

- It's where companies seek growth.
- Where investors seek opportunity.
- Where institutions deploy strategy.
- Where regulators enforce fairness.
- And where you, the thoughtful individual, can carve your space.

You don't need to know everything that's happening. But you do need to know where it's happening—and who else is in the room.

The more clearly you see the field, the less likely you are to panic during the game.

One-Line Summary

The stock market isn't a chaotic mess—it's a structured field with visible players, invisible forces, and consistent rules. Know the field, and you stop feeling lost.

Chapter 8: The Price Is Not the Value

How perception drives prices and how to see deeper than the number.

You open your investing app. You see a company's stock price: $82.45. You wonder, "Is it cheap or expensive?" Someone says, "It's down 30%! Grab it." Another says, "That stock? Overhyped trash." A finance show calls it "undervalued." Your friend says it'll double next month.

Confused yet?

Welcome to one of the oldest paradoxes in the market:

The price you see is not the value you get.

This is one of the most important mental models every investor must master. Because if you mistake price for value, you'll end up buying noise and selling potential.

Let's unpack what this really means—and how it separates wise investors from frantic traders.

1. Price Is What You Pay. Value Is What You Get.

This famous quote by Warren Buffett says it best:

"Price is what you pay. Value is what you get."

Let's take it out of the stock market for a second.

Imagine you're buying a pair of shoes.

- One is priced at ₹5,000, made with high-quality materials, built to last 3 years.

- Another is ₹2,000, looks great, but wears out in 3 months.

Which is the better deal?

If you only look at price, you choose the cheaper one. But if you consider value, you realize the more expensive one actually offers more utility per rupee.

That's the essence of investing too.

In the market, price is just the latest number someone was willing to pay. Value is what the company is fundamentally worth based on its assets, earnings, potential, and strength.

2. Why Price and Value Often Disagree

If the market were perfectly rational, price and value would always match. But it's not. Why?

Because price is influenced by perception—and perception is emotional, noisy, and short-sighted.

Value is grounded in fundamentals—earnings, growth, products, leadership.

But price? It changes second by second based on:

- News
- Rumors
- Social media
- Analyst ratings
- Global trends
- Sentiment
- Fear
- Greed

A great company might fall in price because of market panic. A terrible company might rise because of a trending tweet.

This gap between price and value is what creates opportunity—but also confusion.

As an investor, your job is not to chase price movements. Your job is to recognize value *beneath* the surface.

3. Mispricing: The Market's Imperfect Mirror

The market is a reflection of what people believe a company is worth. But beliefs aren't always accurate.

This leads to two common situations:

Undervaluation

When the price is lower than what the business is truly worth. Smart investors often spot this, buy in, and wait for the market to "correct" the price upward.

Overvaluation

When the price is higher than the company's real performance or potential justifies. Happens often during hype cycles—when people pay more for *hope* than for *reality*.

Mispricing isn't a bug in the market—it's a feature.

It's how calm, long-term players earn outsized returns: By buying value when others are obsessing over price.

4. How to Look Beyond the Price Tag

You don't need to be a financial analyst to sense value. But you do need a system for evaluating a company beyond the number on your screen.

Here are five simple questions to ask:

a) What does the company actually do?

Is it solving a real problem? Does it have a product or service with demand?

b) Is it making money—or at least building toward it?

Check revenue, profit trends, and debt levels. Is it growing, flat, or shrinking?

c) Who runs it?

Leadership matters. A great product can fail with bad management.

d) Is the price reasonable relative to what it earns?

This is where metrics like P/E ratio (Price to Earnings) come in. A stock trading at 80 times earnings is far more expensive than one at 15—*if both are growing equally.*

e) Can it survive a storm?

Look for strong balance sheets, loyal customers, diversified operations. Value isn't just potential—it's also resilience.

Price is visible. Value requires vision.

The more you train yourself to ask these questions, the less price-driven you become—and the more value-aligned you grow.

5. Real-World Examples: Price ≠ Value

Let's look at two simplified scenarios:

Company A: Tech Titan in Panic

- Known for consistent profits.
- Just released strong earnings.
- But the overall market fell 10% due to global panic.

- Its stock drops from $100 to $85.

Here, price fell, but the company's value didn't change.
In fact, it may now be a better deal than before.

Company B: Biotech Hype

- No profits yet. Just a promising trial.
- Social media buzz goes wild.
- Stock shoots from $10 to $25 in 3 weeks.

Here, price jumped, but value may not have justified it—especially if results don't hold up.
The difference?
A wise investor sees through the fog. A hype-chaser only sees the number.

6. Market Cycles: When the World Forgets Value

Entire markets go through phases where price and value separate wildly:

Bull Markets (Over-Excitement Phase)

- Prices rise rapidly.
- Everyone feels like a genius.
- Valuations lose meaning.
- "Buy high" becomes the norm.
- Value gets ignored—until reality hits.

Bear Markets (Over-Fear Phase)

- Prices fall even for healthy companies.
- People panic-sell good assets.
- "All stocks are bad" becomes the mood.
- Value hides in plain sight—waiting for patient players.

The best investors don't swing with the crowd. They observe the crowd—and make independent calls based on intrinsic value, not market mood.

7. Investing vs. Speculating: A Value Perspective

The Speculator asks:

- "Will the price go up soon?"
- "What's the buzz this week?"
- "How can I double my money fast?"

The Investor asks:

- "Is this business worth owning at this price?"
- "Where will this company be in five years?"
- "Does this valuation make sense based on fundamentals?"

See the shift?
Speculation is driven by short-term price action. Investing is driven by long-term value conviction.
Both can be profitable. But only one is sustainable.

8. Cultivating a Value Mindset: How to Train Your Eye

You're not born seeing value—you learn it.
Here's how to build your value radar:

- Read company annual reports. Slowly. One at a time.
- Follow 2–3 long-term investors—not traders. Observe how they think.
- Use basic valuation tools: P/E ratio, earnings growth, debt levels.
- Ask "What am I buying *into*?" instead of "What am I buying *at*?"

And most importantly: Detach from the stock price momentarily. Look at the business, not just the stock.
You're not buying a lottery ticket. You're partnering with a business.

Final Thought: Your Calm Is Your Edge

In a world where prices blink by the second and headlines scream for attention, value investors move slowly.
They don't look smart immediately. Sometimes, they even look wrong—for a while.
But over time, the market catches up.
Because in the long run, the market is a weighing machine, not a voting machine.
It eventually rewards substance over popularity, performance over perception, truth over trend.
And those who saw value before the crowd?
They don't just win. They win quietly—and consistently.

One-Line Summary

The stock price is just the surface—value is what lies underneath. Learn to see deeper than the number, and you'll stop reacting, start reasoning.

Interlude

You Know the Rules—Now Trust Yourself to Play

Let's take a breath.

You've made it through Level 2—and that's no small thing.

Most people who enter the market don't bother learning the rules. They rush in. They chase tips. They react to prices. They confuse hype with insight, and confusion with risk.

But you?

You paused. You reflected. You understood what's beneath the surface.

You've learned that:

- The market is not magic—it's a system.
- Time is not just a measure—it's a strategy.
- Risk is not the enemy—it's the energy of reward.
- Your mind is not neutral—it's full of hidden biases.
- Price is not value—and knowing the difference is power.

You're no longer walking into this world blind. You see the field. You hear the noise—but you're not ruled by it. You've sharpened your lens.

That makes you rare.

You now know how the game is played—so you can stop guessing, and start thinking.

The next level is about **action**. Not rash moves—but thoughtful steps. Not "winning," but *beginning.*

You'll learn how to choose, how to buy, how to build. But more importantly, how to **stay in the game**—your game.

You don't need perfect timing.

You don't need insider knowledge.

You don't need to get rich quick.

You just need:

- A steady mind
- A simple plan
- And the courage to make your first move

So when you're ready—Level 3 awaits.

Level 3: Making Your Moves

Chapter 9: How to Buy Your First Share

Accounts, brokers, steps, and that magical first "buy."

So, you've made it this far.

You understand the game. You know the rules. You've seen through the noise. And now, you're ready to do something most people never do—not because they can't, but because they never feel *ready enough.*

You're ready to buy your first share.

Let's begin not with urgency, but with clarity.

Because this moment isn't about chasing profits. It's about making a move that aligns with your new mindset.

Think of it as your first step into a broader world—not just as a buyer, but as a business participant. You're about to become a co-owner (even if just by a fraction) of something real.

This chapter will walk you through every detail—what accounts you need, how to choose a broker, how to place that first order, and most importantly—how to feel calm, confident, and clear while doing it.

Step 1: Set Up the Foundation – Your Investment Accounts

Before you can invest, you need to open two essential accounts:

1. Demat Account (Dematerialized Account)

This is where your shares are stored electronically—just like money in a bank. No physical certificates. No paperwork flying around. Your ownership is held in digital form.

Think of it as your locker.

2. Trading Account

This is your interface with the market. It allows you to place buy and sell orders. It connects your Demat account to the stock exchange through your broker.

Usually, your broker will help you open both at once as part of a single onboarding process.

Note: In some countries (like the U.S.), the concept of a separate Demat account may not exist. Brokers like Robinhood or Fidelity hold your shares for you under custodial arrangements. In India, however, Demat and trading accounts are distinct.

Step 2: Choose Your Broker – Your Bridge to the Market

A broker is a registered intermediary that allows you to access the stock exchange. They don't decide what you buy—they just enable it.

What to Look for in a Broker

- **Ease of Use:** Clean app or website interface
- **Costs:** Low brokerage fees, especially if you're starting small
- **Security:** Licensed, well-known, regulated platforms
- **Support:** Responsive customer service and educational tools

- **Extras (Optional):** Research reports, charting tools, stock screeners

Popular Brokers Around the World

India:

- Zerodha
- Groww
- Upstox
- ICICI Direct
- Angel One

United States:

- Robinhood
- Charles Schwab
- Fidelity
- TD Ameritrade
- E*TRADE

Global:

- eToro
- Interactive Brokers
- Saxo Bank

Pro Tip: Start with a platform you *enjoy using*. You'll build confidence faster when the app or website feels intuitive.

Step 3: Complete KYC and Account Setup

Once you've chosen your broker, you'll need to complete a basic identity verification process—this varies slightly by country but typically includes:

- Government-issued ID (passport, PAN card, driver's license)
- Address proof (utility bill, bank statement)
- Bank account details for fund transfers
- Photograph and digital signature
- Income declaration (some brokers ask for this before enabling derivatives or higher-risk instruments)

This is usually a one-time process. Once approved, your trading and Demat accounts will be ready—often within 24–48 hours.

Step 4: Add Funds to Your Trading Account

This is your first transaction—but not your first investment yet.
Transfer money from your bank account into your trading account. Most platforms offer:

- Instant bank transfer (UPI/ACH/NEFT)
- Debit card or payment gateway
- Scheduled deposits (auto-invest, SIP-style)

Start small. Even $10 or ₹500 is enough to begin. This is a psychological move more than a financial one. It tells your brain: *I've entered the game.*

Step 5: Research Your First Stock

Before clicking "buy," stop and think.
This is your *first share.* Let it be one you actually understand.

Pick a stock using these beginner-friendly filters:

- Is it a brand you recognize or use?
- Do you understand how it makes money?
- Has the business been around for a while?
- Is the stock price relatively stable (not overly volatile)?
- Has it shown consistent growth or profitability?

Examples (not recommendations):

- Consumer goods (FMCG) companies
- Blue-chip stocks (large, well-established firms)
- Tech platforms you believe in
- Bank stocks with steady returns
- ETFs or Index Funds for broader exposure

Don't overthink. Your first share doesn't have to be perfect. It just needs to be intentional.
Think of it as planting your first tree—not designing the entire forest.

Step 6: Placing the Buy Order – Your First Real Move

This is the big moment. Here's what to do.

Go to your broker's trading dashboard

Search for the stock you've chosen—by name or symbol (e.g., INFY, AAPL, TATASTEEL).

Click "Buy" – You'll see a simple form

You'll be asked for:

- **Quantity** – Number of shares you want to buy
- **Price Type** –
    - Market Order (buy at the current price instantly)
    - Limit Order (set your own price—order executes only if price matches)
- **Order Validity** –
    - Day Order (expires end of day)
    - GTC – Good Till Cancelled (if supported)

For your first order, just use:

- Market Order
- 1 or 2 shares
- Day Validity

Review and Click "Confirm"

Congratulations—you just bought your first share.
No fanfare. No music. But internally? You just crossed a threshold. You're no longer just reading about markets. You're in it.

You didn't just buy a stock—you took responsibility for your financial future.

Step 7: Where Does It Go?

After your order is executed:

- The shares will reflect in your Demat account within T+1 or T+2 days (depending on your country and exchange rules).
- You'll get an order confirmation, a contract note, and an updated portfolio view in your app.
- You can now see that you *own* a real piece of a business.

You can track the price, view reports, and watch how it performs—but resist the urge to check it every 10 minutes.
Your job is done. Let the company work. Let time work.

Step 8: What You Should Feel (And What You Shouldn't)

You may feel excitement. You may feel fear. You might even refresh your app repeatedly just to "see how it's doing."
That's normal.
But remember:

- One stock won't make you rich.
- One red day doesn't mean it's failing.
- You're building a relationship, not trading attention.
- This is just one step on a long path.

Take a screenshot. Write a journal entry. Capture this moment. Because one day, you'll look back and smile at how it all began—with a single click, powered by quiet conviction.

A Word on Mistakes

What if the stock drops? What if you picked the wrong one? Here's the thing: you will make mistakes in this game. Everyone does. That's not failure—it's tuition.

Your first few trades aren't about returns. They're about learning how you react.

Investing is not about always being right. It's about building the habits that keep you in the game—even when you're wrong.

So breathe easy. Celebrate your start. You're ahead of 90% of people who talk about investing but never actually begin.

Checklist: Your First Share Journey

- [ ] Chose a regulated, trustworthy broker
- [ ] Opened Demat + trading account
- [ ] Transferred small capital to start
- [ ] Picked a company with purpose
- [ ] Placed first buy order
- [ ] Reflected on the experience
- [ ] Didn't panic (or at least not too much!)

One-Line Summary

Buying your first share isn't just a transaction—it's a quiet declaration that you're ready to participate, not just observe.

Chapter 10: Don't Build a Portfolio

Build a Philosophy

Your strategy matters more than your spreadsheet.

After buying your first share, something begins to shift. You feel the urge to do more. To build. To "fill in the blanks." You start wondering:

- "What's next?"
- "How many stocks should I have?"
- "Should I buy one in tech? One in finance? One in energy?"
- "How do I diversify properly?"
- "What should my allocation be?"

These are good questions. They're part of the natural curiosity that comes with growth.

But hold on.

Before you build a portfolio, ask a deeper question:

What kind of investor do I want to be?

Because without a guiding philosophy, your portfolio will become a collection of confusion—a buffet of opinions, trends, and second-hand advice.

This chapter is your anchor. It's not about how many stocks to own or what sectors to chase. It's about something much more foundational: Your philosophy—the filter through which every decision is made.

What Is an Investment Philosophy?

An investment philosophy is your personal rulebook. It defines:

- How you think about money
- How you choose what to buy
- How long you hold
- What you avoid
- When you exit
- And how you react when the market tests you (and it *will*)

It's like a compass. It doesn't predict the weather, but it ensures you're walking in the right direction—even in fog.
Without a philosophy, you'll always borrow someone else's conviction—and abandon it when things go south.

The Portfolio Trap: Why Buying More Isn't Always Better

There's a common misconception in early investing:
"If I have more stocks, I'm more diversified. And if I'm more diversified, I'm safer."
Not necessarily.
A portfolio without a strategy is like a playlist without a theme. It might be full—but it doesn't say anything about you.
Here's what often happens:

- You buy one stock because of a news article.
- Another because a friend suggested it.
- Another because it "looked cheap."
- Another because it "might be the next Tesla."
- Another because it's "a defensive sector."

You end up with 15–20 stocks—but no real reasoning behind them.
This creates:

- Mental clutter (you don't really know what you own)
- Emotional stress (each red day feels like 20 fires)
- Inconsistent results (you chase gains, avoid learning)

The truth?
You can have five well-chosen stocks with clarity and outperform someone with 25 random ones driven by confusion.

Your Philosophy > Your Quantity

Let's meet two types of investors:

Investor A: The Quantity Seeker

- Owns 30+ stocks
- Adds new ones every week
- Has no clear sell plan
- Reacts to news, trends, fear
- Doesn't review portfolio regularly
- FOMO-driven, scattered focus

- Thinks activity = progress

Investor B: The Philosophy Seeker

- Has 8–12 well-researched positions
- Knows why each one is in their portfolio
- Updates decisions quarterly, not impulsively
- Holds based on business fundamentals, not mood
- Allocates based on conviction
- Accepts volatility as part of the process
- Thinks clarity = power

Guess who performs better in the long run—not just financially, but mentally?
It's not about what you hold. It's about why you hold it.

How to Build Your Philosophy (Before Your Portfolio)

Here's a set of reflective prompts to help define your investing identity.
1. Why are you investing at all?
We've touched this before, but now it gets specific.

- Are you investing for retirement?
- To build wealth slowly over decades?
- To beat inflation?
- To support your kids' education?
- To create financial independence?

Your answer should shape your horizon and risk appetite.

2. What matters more to you—growth or stability?

- Do you prefer exciting high-growth companies with potential ups and downs?
- Or do you lean toward slow, steady compounders?
- Or do you want a mix?

This determines your comfort with volatility.
You can't want high returns and panic every time the price falls 10%. Philosophy means aligning expectations with reality.
3. What type of companies do you believe in?
Start here:

- Companies you understand
- Brands you use
- Industries you can learn about

Avoid exotic sectors you can't explain.
"If I can't explain why I own this to a 12-year-old, I probably shouldn't own it."
This is circle of competence thinking—an essential pillar of any philosophy.
4. What's your ideal holding period—realistically?
Are you someone who:

- Believes in long-term compounding (5–10+ years)?
- Likes medium-term bets (1–3 years)?
- Wants flexibility but not frequent movement?

There's no one right answer. But being honest with yourself saves you from self-sabotage later.

5. How often will you review your holdings?

- Weekly?
- Monthly?
- Quarterly?

Too frequent—and you risk becoming emotional. Too rare—and you risk missing shifts.
Set a rhythm. Your portfolio is like a garden. It needs observation, not obsession.

Building a Philosophy Protects You From These Traps:

◈ Following "hot tips"

You'll pause and ask, "Does this fit my criteria?"

◈ Reacting emotionally to price swings

You'll remember your reason for entering—and stick to it.

◈ Over-diversifying

You'll add new stocks based on *thesis*, not *FOMO*.

◈ Comparing constantly

You'll stop treating investing like a race and more like a personal mission.

Different Philosophies, Same Foundation

Let's be clear—there's no single correct investment philosophy. But the best ones share these traits:

Philosophy Type	Core Belief	Style
Value Investing	Buy great companies at fair or cheap prices	Long-term, low turnover
Growth Investing	Bet on fast-growing companies early	Higher volatility, high conviction
Index Investing	Trust in the whole market to grow over time	Passive, consistent
Dividend Investing	Prefer regular income from shares	Lower volatility, income-focused
Thematic Investing	Believe in specific future trends (AI, green energy, etc.)	Trend-driven, concentrated bets

Your job isn't to pick one perfectly—it's to choose consciously. You can even combine philosophies, as long as you're clear about the why behind each move.

Write Your Investment Constitution

Here's a simple exercise: Write down your Personal Investing Philosophy—your "constitution."
It could be 5–10 bullet points like:

- I only invest in businesses I understand.
- I don't chase hype or trade based on fear.
- I hold for at least 3 years unless something changes fundamentally.

- I invest monthly, regardless of market mood.
- I diversify across 5–10 companies, not more.
- I trust compounding. I don't overcheck my portfolio.

Stick it on your desk. Read it monthly. It's your mental anchor. Because when markets go wild, philosophies stay calm.

From Portfolio Management to Self-Management

Most people think portfolio building is about picking stocks. But really, it's about managing *yourself.*

The more you know your philosophy, the fewer decisions you'll regret. And the more consistent your behavior, the better your long-term outcome.

The goal is not to have the *most* stocks. It's to have a clear relationship with each one—and with yourself.

One-Line Summary

A portfolio shows what you own. A philosophy shows who you are. Choose the second first—and the first will follow with purpose.

Chapter 11: Short-Term Thrills vs. Long-Term Gains

Trading vs. investing. Choose your style—or blend wisely.

You've set up your account. You've bought your first stock. You've started shaping your philosophy.

And then—your screen flashes green. Your stock is up 3% in a day. You feel good. A rush. Maybe a little proud. The next day, it drops 2%. Your mood dips. You refresh again. And again.

Suddenly, you're watching the screen more than the business. You're reacting. Wondering. Calculating.

"Should I just sell now and take the profit?" "Should I buy more before it goes higher?" "Should I enter something else for quicker returns?"

Congratulations. You've now reached a crossroads.

It's a classic tension every new market participant faces:

Am I a trader or an investor? Or something in between?

This chapter will help you understand that difference—not just on the surface, but in the *spirit* of each approach. Because knowing your style of play is just as important as knowing your tools.

Two Games, One Market

Let's get something clear: Trading and investing are not enemies. They're just two different strategies within the same market.

Like sprinting and long-distance running. Same track. Same muscles. Different mindset.

Trading

- Short-term buying and selling of stocks (days, weeks, even minutes)
- Focused on price movements, trends, technical charts
- Requires fast decisions, quick exits, and active attention
- Higher risk, but potentially faster rewards
- Driven by timing

Investing

- Long-term buying and holding of businesses (years, sometimes decades)
- Focused on company fundamentals, growth, dividends, and vision
- Requires patience, conviction, and emotional resilience
- Lower day-to-day stress, more steady wealth building
- Driven by time

So... which one is better?
Wrong question.
The real question is:
Which one fits *you*?

The Psychology Behind Each Style

Let's look under the hood.

Trading Feeds on Action

- Traders enjoy movement.
- They like solving fast puzzles.
- They thrive on energy, speed, and decisive action.
- They seek short-term advantages—price mismatches, volume spikes, pattern setups.

But it comes at a price:

- Constant screen time.
- Emotional fatigue.
- High transaction costs (brokerage, taxes, slippage).
- A lot of small wins—and sudden setbacks.

It's not for the faint-hearted. It's not for the distracted. And it's definitely not for people who can't take being wrong often.

Investing Feeds on Patience

- Investors think like business owners.
- They focus on growth, products, vision, cash flow.
- They don't flinch at every red candle.
- They build wealth slowly, but often more sustainably.

But investing is also hard in its own way:

- It requires *doing nothing* for long stretches.

- It challenges your belief when prices fall.
- It can feel boring while others are "making quick money."

Both trading and investing test your temperament more than your technique.

Understanding the Tools: Different Approaches, Different Metrics

Let's break down what each style focuses on.

Factor	Trader Focus	Investor Focus
Time Horizon	Hours to weeks	Years to decades
Data Used	Technical analysis (charts, indicators)	Fundamental analysis (financials, business model)
Goal	Capitalize on price moves	Grow wealth through business ownership
Risk	High and frequent	Controlled and spread over time
Tools	Candlestick patterns, RSI, moving averages	Balance sheet, earnings reports, management quality
Decision Drivers	Price patterns, volume spikes	Valuation, growth potential, industry trends

Both require skill. But one is attention-intensive. The other is patience-intensive.
Choose wisely.

Which One Should *You* Choose?

Let's assess a few real-world profiles.

Amit, a full-time employee

- Works 9–6, limited screen time
- Wants steady long-term growth
- Doesn't like daily price drama

Ideal Style: Investing

Sara, a curious learner

- Loves charts and fast-paced challenges
- Has time, but also wants structure
- Gets energized by volatility—but hates chaos

Possible Style: Part-time trading with risk limits

Ravi & Nisha, parents saving for their children's future

- Think in decades
- Want consistent, safe compounding
- Prefer simplicity over constant involvement

Ideal Style: Long-term investing + index funds

Nina, a tech-savvy young professional

- Mixes confidence with caution

- Wants growth but is curious about trends
- Not obsessed with screens, but loves data

Blend Style: Core investing + a small trading sandbox
Your *lifestyle* and *personality* should guide your approach—not just your greed or fear.

Blending the Styles: Yes, It's Possible

You don't have to swear loyalty to one camp forever.
You can blend—*as long as you separate your strategies clearly.*

Here's a simple way to structure it:

Core Portfolio (80–90%) – Investor Mode

- Long-term holdings in companies you understand and believe in
- Managed calmly, reviewed quarterly
- Driven by goals, not market noise

Satellite Portfolio (10–20%) – Trader Mode

- Small capital for trend-based positions
- Clearly defined entry/exit strategies
- Treated like practice—not gambling

This way, you satisfy your curiosity without compromising your core.
But never let the satellite become the spaceship. When short-term thrills start driving long-term mistakes, you're off course.

How to Decide—Ask These Questions

Before you declare your style, reflect:

- Do I check prices hourly or quarterly?
- Do I enjoy fast decisions or deliberate ones?
- Do I want activity or clarity?
- Do I get anxious if I don't take action?
- Do I handle losses with logic or with regret?
- Am I looking for income, excitement, or independence?

There's no wrong answer—only an honest one.

The Real Danger: Confused Strategy

Here's what you want to avoid:

- Buying like an investor, but panicking like a trader
- Trading like a gambler, then blaming the market
- Changing your plan mid-way without reflection
- Copying someone else's strategy with none of their context

The worst style is no style. The worst portfolio is one that has no owner—only impulses.
You're not here to impress anyone. You're here to play *your* game.

Key Takeaways:

- Trading = Timing-based, fast, high-risk, high-reward

- Investing = Time-based, slow, resilient, compounding-driven
- Know your personality, schedule, risk appetite
- Don't mix styles emotionally—separate them consciously
- A blended approach works if managed with boundaries

Final Analogy: The Chessboard vs. the Casino

Think of trading like speed chess. Every second counts. You need pattern recognition, quick judgment, and strong nerves.

Investing is like classic chess. It's thoughtful. Strategic. Less about reacting, more about positioning.

Both are games. But only one fits your temperament.

And sometimes, the wisest move is to *not make one until you're sure.*

One-Line Summary

Whether you chase speed or build slowly, know which game you're playing—because thrill fades, but clarity compounds.

Chapter 12: Choosing Companies Like a Player, Not a Fan

Detach from hype. Invest with business sense, not blind love.

Let's play out a scenario.

You love a brand. You wear its clothes. You use its phone. You follow its founders on social media. Every time someone criticizes the company, you feel personally attacked.

And then one day, you hear this voice in your head:

"I love this company so much... I should buy its stock."

Wait. Pause. Breathe.

That right there is where many investors go wrong—not because the company is bad, but because the reason for investing is emotionally charged, not financially grounded.

This chapter is about learning how to choose businesses wisely, not romantically. It's about building your portfolio like a player—someone who understands the *game*—not a fan cheering from the sidelines, hoping their favorite team wins.

The Fan Mindset: Emotional, Biased, Blind

Let's define what it means to be a *fan-investor*.

Fans invest based on:

- Brand loyalty
- Celebrity endorsements
- Social media trends
- Peer pressure

- Personal use or admiration
- National pride

They believe things like:

- "I use their product every day—it must be a great stock."
- "Everyone's talking about it—it's the future."
- "How can something so popular ever fail?"
- "I love this founder—he's a genius."
- "This company is from my country—I want to support it."

These ideas aren't *entirely* wrong. But they become dangerous when they replace critical thinking with emotional projection. Investing is not about what you love. It's about what you understand.

The Player Mindset: Strategic, Observant, Rational

Now let's define the player.
A player-investor doesn't just ask:
"Do I like this company?"
They ask:
"Is this business making money, growing, and priced fairly?"
Players view companies as living businesses, not as badges of loyalty.
They study products, customers, revenue streams, leadership, debt, scalability.

They may admire a brand, but they only invest if the business case makes sense.
Here's the truth:

- A company can have millions of users and still lose money.
- A brand can dominate media and still be drowning in debt.
- A founder can be charismatic and still burn investor cash.

Players detach emotionally so they can think clearly. Fans fall in love—and lose money when love turns blind.

Fan Investing Gone Wrong: A Case Study

Let's look at a classic mistake:

The Scenario:

- A flashy tech startup goes public.
- It's all over the news. The founder is on magazine covers.
- Everyone at your office uses the app.
- You think, "This is the next big thing."
- You buy the stock at ₹800.
- The next few months, it crashes to ₹400.
- You hold on—because you "believe" in it.
- It drops to ₹150.
- You say, "But I use it daily! It's popular!"
- Eventually, it delists.

This has happened before—and will happen again. Because popularity ≠ profitability. And brand loyalty ≠ business fundamentals.

How to Choose Like a Player: The 6-Filter Framework

Let's shift now. Here's a simple checklist to help you evaluate any stock like a rational investor—not a brand fan.

1. What Does the Company Actually Do?

Can you explain its business model in one or two sentences? If not, you're not investing—you're just gambling politely.

- How does it earn money?
- Who are its customers?
- What's its core product or service?

If the business model is too complicated or hidden behind buzzwords—be cautious.

2. Is It Profitable—or Growing Toward Profit?

Check:

- Net income (profit after expenses)
- Operating margins
- Year-on-year revenue and profit growth

Early-stage companies may not be profitable yet—but they should at least show a clear path to profitability.

A loss-making company isn't automatically bad—but if losses keep growing with no sign of improvement, it's a red flag.

3. Who's Running the Show?

Management matters more than marketing.
Check:

- Background and experience of the CEO/founders
- Past performance in other businesses
- Skin in the game (do they own shares?)
- Decision-making style during crises

A good business with a bad captain can still hit the rocks.

4. What's the Financial Health?

Look at:

- Debt-to-equity ratio (how much debt is used to run operations)
- Free cash flow (money left after expenses and capital investments)
- Return on equity (ROE) – How efficiently profits are being generated

Too much debt? Poor cash management? Even a great brand can crumble without financial discipline.

5. Is It Overpriced Right Now?

Even a great company can be a bad buy—if you pay too much.
Use valuation tools like:

- P/E Ratio – Price divided by earnings
- PEG Ratio – P/E divided by growth rate
- Compare with industry peers

A ₹100 stock may be cheaper than a ₹20 one—if it has stronger earnings per share.

6. Does This Fit Your Philosophy?

- Are you buying it for long-term compounding?
- Or for short-term momentum?
- Does it align with your risk appetite?
- Will you be able to sleep at night owning it?

Not every good company is a good buy—for *you*.

How to Handle Companies You Love

So what if you *do* love a brand and want to invest in it?
That's okay.
But treat it like this:

- Double-check the fundamentals. Don't invest just because you're a fan.
- Limit your allocation. Don't let emotional picks dominate your portfolio.
- Be willing to sell. If the business weakens—even if you still love the brand—let go.

Love the company? Great. But marry the numbers, not the narrative.

Emotional Triggers to Watch For

Be wary of these thoughts creeping in:

- "Everyone's using this app—it must be worth investing in."
- "This company will never fail—it's too big!"

- "If I don't buy this now, I'll regret it forever."
- "The founder is so inspiring—I trust him completely."
- "It dropped 30%, but I love their ads—let's double down."

Whenever you feel emotionally attached, take a step back and ask:
"Would I buy this if I'd never heard of it before?"
That one question can save you from many mistakes.

Your Job as an Investor: Act Like an Owner

When you buy a stock, you become a part-owner of the company.

- Would you buy a shop without looking at its finances?
- Would you invest in a restaurant just because you like their decor?
- Would you partner with someone without checking their track record?

Probably not.
So don't do it with public companies either.
Ownership is not admiration. Ownership is responsibility.

Final Thought: The Market Doesn't Reward Emotion—It Rewards Clarity

Fans buy because they want to feel good. Players buy because they want to own good businesses.
You're here to play this game well—not just to cheer from the sidelines.

Detach. Assess. Think. Then click "Buy."
That's how pros are made.

One-Line Summary

You can love a company without owning its stock—and you can own a stock without loving the company. That clarity makes all the difference.

Chapter 13: Every Move Doesn't Have to Be Brilliant

Perfection is the enemy of progress. Keep playing.

Let's begin with a truth no one tells you when you enter the stock market:

You don't need to be brilliant to succeed.

You don't need to find the next Tesla. You don't need to buy at the absolute bottom. You don't need to sell right at the peak. You don't need to beat the market every quarter.

But here's the twist: Everyone thinks they do.

They get caught in what we call the Perfection Trap—the belief that to succeed, every move must be flawless, every pick must be golden, and every exit must be timed with clockwork precision.

Let's destroy that myth now.

Because perfectionism in investing doesn't just slow you down—it burns you out.

This chapter is about embracing imperfection. About showing up, not showing off. About learning to stay in the game—even when your moves aren't magical.

The Myth of the "Genius Investor"

The media loves genius. You'll hear about the person who turned ₹5,000 into ₹5 lakhs. The teen who "called" the crash. The guy who bought Apple in 1998 and never sold.

But what you don't hear is:

- How many mistakes they made before that one success
- How much luck played a role
- How often they underperformed afterward
- How their psychology was shaped over years of losses and learning

The myth of genius investing creates an invisible pressure:
"If I'm not crushing it, I must be doing something wrong."
Wrong.
The market is not an exam. It's a marathon. And you don't need to be a top scorer—you just need to finish strong.

Why Perfectionism Hurts Your Progress

Let's break down how perfection thinking poisons your journey:

1. Analysis Paralysis

You overthink every decision:

- "Is this the perfect entry point?"
- "Should I wait for a dip?"
- "What if I buy and it drops?"
- "Is there a better stock I haven't discovered yet?"

Result? No action. No progress.
A good decision made calmly beats a perfect one made too late.

2. Fear of Mistakes

You avoid action because you're terrified of being wrong.

But here's the irony:

- Mistakes are how you learn
- Losses are how you sharpen your strategy
- Failing early is better than failing big later

Perfectionists fear loss so much, they miss out on learning curves that build resilience.

3. Overreaction to Small Losses

You make a reasonable move. It dips 5%. You panic. You sell. You feel stupid.

You say, "I knew I wasn't good at this."

But the truth is: You weren't wrong. You were just expecting perfect timing, which no one gets—not even pros.

4. Unrealistic Comparisons

You see someone else:

- Bought a stock that doubled in 3 months
- Made "life-changing" returns on crypto
- Has a fancy dashboard with charts you don't understand

Suddenly, your modest portfolio feels dull. You feel behind.

That's not investing. That's insecurity dressed up as strategy.

The market rewards consistency—not comparison.

What Real Progress Looks Like

Let's shift focus.

You know what successful investing actually looks like?

- Buying steadily, not dramatically
- Holding through noise, not reacting emotionally
- Learning from errors and staying in the game
- Following your plan—even when it's not sexy
- Celebrating patience—not panic-fueled profit

Let's meet Ritu.
Ritu:

- Invests ₹5,000 monthly in 4 companies she understands
- Has held some stocks for 4 years
- Doesn't obsess over daily price
- Missed out on a few "hot" trades—but never lost big
- Grows at 12–15% annually

No fireworks. No headlines. But over 15 years, her net worth grows quietly and confidently.
That's brilliance—disguised as discipline.

The 80/20 of Investing: You Don't Need Every Move to Win

Here's a secret:
In most successful portfolios, a few good decisions do most of the heavy lifting.
This is called the Pareto Principle: 80% of the gains often come from 20% of the moves.
What does that mean for you?

- You can afford to get some things wrong

- You don't have to pick the top winner every year
- You just need to be right enough, long enough

In other words:
You don't have to be perfect—you just have to stay in the game.

A Better Goal: Be Reasonably Right, Repeatedly

Instead of:

- "How do I pick the next big winner?"

Ask:

- "Can I make thoughtful decisions consistently for the next 10 years?"

Instead of:

- "What if I make a mistake?"

Ask:

- "How do I learn from small mistakes to avoid big ones later?"

Instead of:

- "How do I beat the market every quarter?"

Ask:

- "How do I align my actions with my goals, even when the market is irrational?"

These shifts will give you freedom from pressure—and power to persist.

When You Make a Bad Move (Because You Will)

Let's normalize what happens when you mess up.

Scenario:

You buy a stock. It drops 20%. You're confused.

Option 1: Emotional Response

"I'm an idiot. I should never have entered the market. I'll sell everything."

Option 2: Player Response

"Let me check if my reason for buying still holds. If yes, I'll wait. If not, I'll exit and learn."
Perfection says: "You failed." Progress says: "You adjusted."

What to Track Instead of "Perfection"

Don't track brilliance. Track behavior.
Create a simple progress journal:

Date	Move	Why I Did It	What Happened	What I Learned
Jan 10	Bought ABC	Believed in growth, fair value	Fell 8% in 2 weeks	I panicked—next time, give 3 months minimum

These reflections are worth more than your brokerage reports. They turn you from a spectator into a strategist.

A Player's Philosophy on Progress

Here's what players believe:

- "Some moves will fail. I'll recover."
- "Not every dip is a mistake."
- "Progress = showing up consistently, not perfectly."
- "Losses are tuition—not punishment."
- "It's better to be steady than spectacular."

They don't chase brilliance. They build endurance.

Perfection is Loud. Progress is Quiet.

Perfection is:

- Flashy
- Performance-driven
- External (comparison-based)
- High-pressure

Progress is:

- Subtle
- Process-driven
- Internal (self-aware)
- Peaceful

One keeps you anxious. The other keeps you in the game.
Choose wisely.

Final Thought: Keep Playing

You're not here to be a market prophet. You're not here to be a genius picker. You're here to play.
One move won't define you. But your discipline will shape your future.
Don't aim for brilliance. Aim for resilience.
That's how real investors are made.

One-Line Summary

The market doesn't demand perfection—it rewards those who stay honest, steady, and in the game long enough to let progress do its work.

Interlude

You've Moved—Now You Must Endure

Let's pause again.

Because what you just did is more than just click buttons or read advice. You've crossed the line between theory and practice. Between dreaming and doing.

You:

- Opened your account
- Made your first investment
- Started asking better questions
- Faced your own fears and perfectionism
- Built a philosophy, not just a portfolio

You didn't wait to become an expert. You didn't chase a shortcut. You played the game with **intention**.

And that makes you rare.

Now comes the hardest part—**not quitting**.

Because most people don't fail at investing due to lack of intelligence. They fail because they can't endure:

- Boredom
- Doubt
- Fear
- Noise
- Comparison

But you can.

Because you've built something stronger than luck—you've built **clarity**.

You no longer need to chase brilliance. You just need to stay present, stay patient, and stay in the game.

The next level is where the real difference is made.

It's about staying calm when the market screams. It's about tuning out noise without tuning out reality. It's about evolving your thinking as your money—and mind—mature.

You've made your moves.

Now let's learn how to **last**.

Level 4: Staying In The Game

Chapter 14: Scoreboard Watching Will Kill You

Why daily price-checking leads to emotional burnout.

You've entered the game.

Your first shares are in place. Your portfolio is taking shape. You've built a philosophy, made some moves—and then it begins.

You check your phone. Refresh the app. Look at the prices. It's green! You smile. It's red! You frown. You check again. And again. Every hour. Every coffee break. Before bed. First thing in the morning.

You're not trading.

But your mind is.

This chapter is about the hidden danger most new investors face after they begin:

Obsessing over the scoreboard.

It feels harmless. It feels responsible. It even feels like progress.

But in truth, constant price-checking is the slowest way to kill your confidence, clarity, and calm.

Let's understand why.

The Psychology Behind Refresh Addiction

Why do we keep checking prices?

Because price movement triggers emotion.

- A little green gives us a dopamine hit: *"I'm doing*

well!"

- A little red sets off cortisol: *"Am I messing up?"*
- Flat days feel like boredom: *"Should I be doing more?"*

What's really happening?
You've trained your brain to associate investing with instant feedback—a loop of stimulus and reaction. It becomes a mini casino in your pocket. A never-ending scoreboard.
And here's the catch:
The more frequently you check your portfolio, the less rational you become.

The Feedback Loop of Emotional Overload

Let's play this out.

Day 1

You buy a stock at ₹500. You feel excited, hopeful.

Day 2

It's ₹490. You feel nervous. "Was it a mistake?"

Day 3

Back to ₹505. You feel smart again. "I knew it."

Day 4

₹475. You panic. "Why is it falling? Should I sell?"
None of these prices mean anything fundamentally.
But to your brain, they feel like constant judgment:

- Are you right or wrong?
- Winning or losing?
- Smart or stupid?

It's exhausting. And unnecessary.
The market tests your money occasionally—but it tests your mind daily.

Daily Prices ≠ Daily Progress

Here's a truth most investors forget:
Businesses don't grow—or collapse—every 5 minutes.
So why do you track them like they do?
Stock prices move all the time because of:

- Market liquidity
- Algorithmic trades
- News flow
- Sector momentum
- Global cues
- Investor emotion

But the company itself—its revenue, leadership, customers—doesn't change every hour.
◈ A bakery doesn't change its business health just because its stock drops ₹5.
◈ A software company's R&D value doesn't evaporate because someone sold a few thousand shares.
When you over-watch prices, you under-trust the process.

What Constant Checking Actually Does to You

Let's name the consequences—because they're real.

1. Emotional Burnout

Your mood begins to swing with the market. Red = panic. Green = euphoria. Flat = impatience.

This leads to chronic anxiety and loss of focus.

2. Impulsive Behavior

You see a small dip and react. You overtrade. You "adjust" your portfolio without clarity.

The result? You break your own strategy.

3. Shallow Thinking

You stop thinking about businesses. You only think about prices.

Instead of:

"How is this company performing?"

You think:

"Why is it down ₹8 today?"

You're no longer investing. You're just spectating—from the sidelines of your own portfolio.

4. Comparison Syndrome

You check your stocks. Then you check someone else's.

You feel behind. You get envious. You question your process.

Comparison poisons progress.

5. Loss of Joy

What began as curiosity and confidence becomes fear management.

You dread market open. You check pre-market movement at 9:00 AM. You scroll before bed. You dream in candlesticks.

That's not strategy. That's emotional servitude.

Zooming Out: What the Data Actually Says

Let's look at long-term investing wisdom.
The more frequently you check your portfolio:

- The more losses you'll *see*
- The more decisions you'll *doubt*
- The more trades you'll *make*
- The more fees you'll *pay*
- The more returns you'll lose

Why?

Because short-term volatility feels bigger than it is when viewed up close.
A 5% dip in one week feels like a collapse. Zoomed out over 5 years, it's a tiny bump on a long highway.
Imagine reading a novel by zooming in on each word, every second. You'd never enjoy the story. You'd just exhaust yourself.
The market is no different.

What to Do Instead: Observation Without Obsession

Let's get practical.
You don't need to be blind to your portfolio. You just need to build a healthy rhythm.
Here's how:
1. Set a Portfolio Check Schedule

- Beginner Investor: Once a month
- Experienced Investor: Once every 2–4 weeks

- Long-Term Holder: Once per quarter

Use these sessions to:

- Review fundamentals
- Read company updates
- Reassess your goals

Not to react to prices.

2. Turn Off Unnecessary Notifications

Disable:

- Daily price alerts
- Stock news buzzers
- App updates for every micro-movement

If it's urgent, you'll hear it in your review window.

3. Create a "Hold Journal"

Write a one-liner for each stock:
"I own this because ______."
When fear kicks in, read that journal.
Your past clarity will save your present from panic.

4. Follow Progress, Not Price

Track things like:

- Quarterly earnings
- Revenue growth
- New products
- Market share gains
- Management commentary

These are business metrics, not just screen flickers.

5. Develop Other Interests

Strange advice in an investing book?
No. It's essential.
If the only thing that gives you a rush is market movement, you'll become a volatility addict.
Work on your skills. Build a side hustle. Read. Create. Let investing support your life—not dominate it.

A Better Metric: Emotional Stability

You know what truly reflects investing maturity?
Not your CAGR. Not your top-performing stock. But your ability to say:
"I haven't checked my portfolio in two weeks—and I'm at peace."
That's strength. That's ownership. That's endurance.
That's when the market stops controlling you—and starts working for you.

Final Analogy: The Farmer vs. the Day Trader

A farmer plants a seed. He waters it. He weeds the land. He waits.
He doesn't dig it up every day to "check if it's growing."
Why?
Because he knows the cycle.
He's not there to control time. He's there to align with it.
You, dear investor, are the same.
You're not managing prices. You're nurturing potential.

Stop digging up your investments to measure them every hour. Let them root. Let them grow. Let them breathe.

One-Line Summary

The scoreboard isn't the game. The price isn't the progress. Check your investments less often—and trust your process more deeply.

Chapter 15: Market Cycles Are Seasons—Not Earthquakes

Understanding booms, busts, and why you shouldn't panic.

Imagine you walk outside one day, and it's raining. Do you assume something is wrong with the planet?

Of course not. It's just weather. Part of a larger, predictable rhythm called seasons.

Spring brings growth. Summer brings abundance. Autumn brings change. Winter brings stillness.

And then it all repeats—again and again.

The market is no different. It has seasons too.

But here's the problem:

Most people treat every market dip like an earthquake—a catastrophic event that must be avoided, escaped, or survived.

They panic. They sell. They run. Why? Because no one ever told them the truth:

Booms and busts are not bugs in the system. They're features of the game.

This chapter is about recognizing the rhythms of the market—so that you stop reacting, and start aligning.

The Four Seasons of the Market

Let's map the market cycle to the seasons of the year. It's not a perfect metaphor—but it's powerful for long-term thinking.

Spring – The Recovery Phase

- Market begins rising after a major drop
- Sentiment slowly shifts from fear to hope
- Economic data starts to improve
- Smart investors begin accumulating

Key Traits:

- Undervalued stocks
- Early signs of confidence
- Low noise, high opportunity

This is where the quiet winners plant their seeds.

Summer – The Growth Phase (Bull Market)

- Prices rise across sectors
- Optimism is everywhere
- Media is filled with success stories
- IPOs boom, and everyone seems to be investing

Key Traits:

- Strong momentum
- Higher risk appetite
- New retail investors enter
- Greed overtakes caution

This is where the crowd joins the game.

Autumn – The Peak and Transition

- Market hits euphoric highs
- Valuations are stretched
- Doubts begin to creep in
- Early warnings appear—but are ignored

Key Traits:

- Volatility increases
- Smart money begins exiting
- Retail optimism turns into overconfidence

This is where complacency becomes expensive.

Winter – The Correction / Crash Phase (Bear Market)

- Prices fall sharply
- Panic selling begins
- Media turns negative
- People leave the market

Key Traits:

- Great businesses become undervalued
- Emotions run high
- Survival feels more important than opportunity

This is where wealth quietly changes hands—from fearful to patient players.

How These Cycles Repeat (Historically and Naturally)

Let's look at examples:

- Dot-com Bubble (2000): Tech euphoria → crash → slow recovery → huge long-term winners like Amazon
- Global Financial Crisis (2008): Economic collapse → policy response → decade-long bull run
- COVID-19 (2020): Sudden crash → explosive rebound → tech boom → correction

Every crash looked like "the end." Every boom looked "unstoppable." And yet, markets kept moving, like seasons changing.
The market always survives. The only question is: Do you?

Why We Treat Cycles Like Crises

Here's why people panic during normal market corrections:
1. Media Amplifies Fear
Headlines like:

- "₹10 lakh investor loses everything!"
- "Markets in turmoil!"
- "Recession looms—should you sell everything?"

These headlines don't serve your portfolio. They serve clicks. News sells panic. But investing requires patience.
2. We Personalize Losses
A red screen feels like a red flag:

- "Did I mess up?"
- "Was this a stupid decision?"
- "What if it goes to zero?"

This leads to emotionally-driven exits—right before the recovery.

3. We Assume Today = Forever

If the market is down today, we assume:

"This is the new normal."

We forget that recoveries are as reliable as crashes.

In fact, every market downturn in history has eventually been followed by a new high.

What a Market Crash Really Means

Let's reframe what happens in a crash:

The Fear View:

- "I'm losing money!"
- "I need to stop the bleeding."
- "This is proof that investing is too risky."

The Player View:

- "Prices are falling faster than value is."
- "Great companies are on discount."
- "This is winter—and I've seen this season before."

Reality Check:

- If the business hasn't changed—but the stock is down

20%—you didn't lose money. You just got a temporary markdown on long-term value.

A dip is not destruction. It's often a discount.

How to Survive—and Thrive—in Every Cycle

1. Know Your Season

Ask:

- Are we in early spring (post-crash recovery)?
- Are we in late summer (overheated market)?
- Is winter coming—or already here?

Your behavior should match the mood of the market—not fight it.

2. Don't Be a Hero—or a Herd

Avoid:

- Trying to time the exact bottom or top
- Following the crowd into every hot trend
- Overexposure during euphoria
- Overreaction during panic

Smart players build consistency across cycles—not drama.

3. Use Crashes as a Checklist

In downturns, review your portfolio:

- Has the business model changed?
- Are earnings collapsing—or just sentiment?
- Is the company adapting to economic shifts?

If nothing's broken—stay in. If something's rotten—reallocate.

4. Keep Cash for Opportunity

Winter is the season of value.

If you have spare cash, this is where it works best—quietly, patiently, and at great entry points.

5. Don't Forget to Rebalance

In long bull runs, some stocks may grow too fast. Your portfolio may become overweight in one sector.

Take time to:

- Trim profits
- Rebalance allocations
- Reduce emotional bias

Discipline is easier when the sun is shining. Use that time wisely.

Final Perspective: You're Not Here for One Season

You're not trying to:

- Win spring
- Master summer
- Avoid autumn
- Survive winter

You're trying to play through decades of cycles. Let others react. You respond.

Farmers don't quit because of one bad season. They plan, adapt, and stay—because they understand the soil.

You are the same.
You're not here for a sprint through summer. You're here to learn the full weather of wealth creation.

Final Analogy: Earthquakes vs. Ecosystems

An earthquake is random, destructive, and rare. It leaves ruin in its wake.
But a season is patterned, natural, and necessary.
The market is not collapsing—it's breathing.
Your job is not to panic during the exhale. Your job is to stay rooted and wait for spring.

One-Line Summary

Markets don't move in straight lines—they breathe in cycles. Understand the seasons, and you'll stop panicking through every passing cloud.

Chapter 16: The Magic Move

Doing Nothing (Sometimes)

Patience as a power move. How compounding quietly wins.

We live in a world that celebrates action.

Move fast. Do more. Hustle. React. Optimize. Execute.

And in that noise, one powerful truth gets buried:

In investing, sometimes the smartest thing you can do is... nothing.

No move. No change. No reaction. No tinkering.

Just... holding. Waiting. Letting time do what time always does: Compound.

This chapter is about embracing inaction as intelligent action. It's about learning to sit still—on purpose, not out of fear or laziness.

Because when you understand how compounding works, you realize:

The move that feels boring today is often the one that creates wealth tomorrow.

Why We Struggle With Doing Nothing

Let's be honest—it's hard.

Inaction feels like indecision. Silence feels like weakness. Waiting feels like failure.

When your stock dips, your brain says:

"Do something!" When your stock rises, your brain says: "Take profit!" When nothing moves, your brain says: "Maybe I picked the wrong one."
We're wired to believe that more effort = better outcome. But in investing, that equation often breaks.
Activity can feel like control. But it often leads to chaos.

The Cost of Over-Doing

Most losses in investing aren't because people picked terrible companies. They're because they:

- Sold too soon
- Re-entered too late
- Moved in and out emotionally
- Over-traded in the name of "management"

Let's call this The Tinkering Tax—the cost you pay for not trusting your own plan.
Here's how it compounds negatively:

- Every trade has transaction costs (commissions, taxes)
- Every sell-and-buy risks emotional timing
- Every re-entry delays compounding
- Every "rebalancing impulse" steals focus from the fundamentals

The market already has enough volatility. Don't add your own.

How Compounding Really Works

Let's revisit the greatest force in long-term investing: compounding.

At its core, compounding is simple:

Your money earns returns → those returns get reinvested → now your returns earn returns

Do that over years, and it creates a snowball.

But here's the secret:

Compounding doesn't reward brilliance. It rewards duration.

The Rule of 72

A simple formula: 72 ÷ your annual return = years to double your money

At 12% per year → your money doubles in 6 years At 15% per year → doubles in ~4.8 years At 8% per year → doubles in 9 years

Now imagine:

- You earn 12%, but you keep exiting and re-entering
- Your real return drops to 8%
- You didn't lose money—but you lost years

Every time you interrupt compounding, you reset the clock.

Inaction ≠ Ignorance. It's Strategy.

Doing nothing is often mistaken for:

- Being passive
- Being uninformed
- Being frozen

But true investing patience is:

- Conscious
- Strategic
- Rooted in long-term thinking

It sounds like:
"I've done my research. I trust this company. I don't need to babysit it daily."
That's not inaction. That's conviction.

What Doing Nothing Looks Like (In Real Life)

1. Holding Through Volatility
You buy a strong stock. It drops 15%. You don't panic. You hold. You wait. A year later, it recovers and doubles.
That's a power move.
2. Letting Winners Run
You bought a stock at ₹200. It's now ₹600. Your friend says:
"Book profit, man. Don't be greedy."
You smile. You do nothing. You let it run. Three years later—it's ₹2,000.
That's how generational wealth is created.
Remember: You don't need to sell just because you're in profit. Let time be your ally, not your exit point.
3. Ignoring Market Noise
Inflation report. Interest rate hikes. Election predictions.
Everyone's adjusting. Panicking. Rebalancing.
You? You check in quarterly. Track company performance. Stay still.
That's not laziness. That's focus.

Real-World Wisdom: What the Greats Say

Warren Buffett:

"The stock market is a device for transferring money from the impatient to the patient."

Charlie Munger:

"The big money is not in the buying or the selling, but in the waiting."

Naval Ravikant:

"Play long-term games with long-term people."
These aren't quotes. They're philosophies. They work because the world rewards longevity more than speed.

Why Time Is Your Greatest Ally

You can't predict markets. You can't control headlines. You can't time everything perfectly.
But you can:

- Stay consistent
- Let winners grow
- Give businesses time to execute
- Avoid unnecessary exits

Time turns average decisions into great ones—if you let it.

When Doing Nothing Is NOT the Right Move

Let's be balanced. Inaction is powerful—but not always wise. Here are moments when you *should* act:

1. Fundamental Breakdown

If the company's earnings collapse, leadership changes, or the product loses relevance—don't wait blindly. Review, and if necessary, exit.

2. If Your Thesis Breaks

You bought a company for its innovation. It stops innovating. Your "why" no longer holds. That's a reason to act.

3. If You Need the Money

Investing is not life insurance. If your financial goals change and you need the funds—sell with strategy, not guilt.

Patience is not stubbornness. It's knowing when to wait—and when to walk.

Build a Process That Protects Patience

Here's a 3-part framework to make "doing nothing" feel smart, not passive.

1. Write Your Investment Thesis

"I bought this company because it has consistent revenue growth, a strong moat, and is fairly valued."

Review it every 6–12 months.

2. Schedule Portfolio Reviews

Once a quarter, check your holdings. Look at:

- Business performance
- New developments
- Risks and opportunities

Outside of that? Let it breathe.

3. Set Holding Triggers

Examples:

- "I will not sell unless the company misses 3 quarters in a row."
- "I will review if the price doubles or halves."
- "No action within 90 days of purchase."

Rules calm emotion.

Final Analogy: The Bamboo and the Oak

A bamboo seed is watered for years—with no visible growth.
Then, in a few weeks, it shoots up 90 feet.
Why?
Because the root system was quietly expanding underground.
Your investments are no different.
You may not see magic weekly. But beneath the surface, value is growing, interest is compounding, businesses are building.
When you try to "help" it grow by digging it up—you ruin it.
Let your portfolio be like a bamboo forest. Rooted. Quiet. Sudden—when the time is right.

One-Line Summary

Sometimes, the strongest move in investing is doing nothing—because time, not timing, is what builds real wealth.

Chapter 17: When to Sell

And When to Sit Still

Exit with clarity. Not panic. Not impulse. Not regret.

Let's be honest.

Selling is harder than buying.

Buying is exciting. Hopeful. Optimistic. Selling? It's heavier. Confusing. Emotional. Even painful.

Sell too early—you miss out on gains. Sell too late—you bleed on the way down. Sell for the wrong reasons—you break your own trust.

And worst of all, you don't know if you were right until much later.

That's why this chapter exists.

To teach you that selling isn't failure—it's a decision. A strategic, sometimes necessary move. But only if made from a place of clarity, not chaos.

This chapter helps you build that clarity.

Let's talk about when to sell, when to sit still, and how to do both with confidence.

Why Selling Is So Emotionally Complicated

Let's break it down.

1. Fear of Missing Out (FOMO)

You sell, and the stock rises another 20%. You feel stupid. Regretful.

Result: Next time, you hesitate to sell—even when you should.

2. Fear of Being Wrong

Selling feels like admitting defeat.

"If I hold, it might recover." "It's only a loss if I sell." "Maybe I'm panicking too soon."

So you hold. And sometimes, things get worse.

3. Emotional Attachment

You fell in love with the brand, the story, the founder.

Selling feels like a breakup.

Even when the business no longer deserves your loyalty, your emotions keep you chained.

4. Overconfidence in Rebound

You think: *"It dropped 30%—it must bounce back!"*

But not all stocks recover. Some fall...and stay there.

Hope is not a strategy. Business reality is.

When to Sell: The 6 Intelligent Triggers

Let's flip the lens.

Here are rational, healthy reasons to exit a position—no panic, no guilt.

1. The Reason You Bought No Longer Exists

You bought because of:

- Strong growth
- Great management
- Unique product
- Consistent earnings

But now:

- Revenue is declining
- Leadership has changed
- Market is shifting
- Company is losing its edge

That's a valid reason to leave.
If your "why" is broken—so is your position.

2. Business Fundamentals Have Deteriorated

Check:

- Consecutive quarters of poor earnings
- Rising debt
- Eroding market share
- Customer base shrinking
- Regulatory trouble

Stocks are not lottery tickets. They're businesses. If the business is clearly weakening—don't wait for the stock to follow.

3. Your Valuation Target Has Been Met (Or Exceeded)

You expected 50% growth over 3 years. The stock delivered that in 8 months.
Now it's overvalued relative to its fundamentals.
You don't need to be greedy.
Sometimes, selling into strength is just harvesting smartly.
You can always reinvest in something with better upside.

4. The Position No Longer Aligns with Your Strategy

You:

- Got more conservative
- Need more liquidity

- Are reallocating to a different sector
- Want to reduce risk exposure

It's okay to change direction as long as you're doing it intentionally, not emotionally.

A thoughtful pivot is not a panic sale. It's portfolio hygiene.

5. You've Found a Better Opportunity

You believe another stock offers:

- Stronger growth
- Lower risk
- Better valuation

And you're moving capital—not because of fear, but because of relative conviction.

Just make sure:

- You're not overtrading
- You're not jumping ship prematurely
- You're comparing apples to apples (same timeframes, same horizon)

6. You Need the Money for Real-Life Reasons

Sometimes, life speaks louder than the market.

- Emergency
- Big purchase
- Change in goals
- Health reasons
- Education

Don't guilt yourself for selling to support your life. That's the point of investing.

When NOT to Sell: The False Alarms

Here's where most investors go wrong.

1. Short-Term Price Drops

You see red. You panic. You sell. Then it rebounds.

Repeat this a few times, and you've created a system that punishes patience.

Volatility ≠ weakness. Learn to hold through noise.

2. Boredom

You've held a stock for 8 months. It hasn't "done anything."

You get impatient. So you sell—not because the company is broken, but because your attention span is.

Not all seeds sprout at the same speed. Let the roots grow.

3. Media Headlines

"Global crash coming!" "Stock XYZ downgraded!" "Recession fears grip market!"

You react.

But headlines are designed to provoke—not guide.

Don't trade your long-term vision for short-term drama.

4. Everyone Else Is Selling

A mass sell-off starts. Prices dip.

You think:

"Everyone's running. Should I?"

Pause.

Ask:

- Has the company changed?
- Is this a market dip—or a business decline?

The crowd rarely times it right. You don't have to join them.

How to Make Peace with Selling

Selling well requires emotional maturity.
Here's how to build that:

Set Exit Criteria Before You Buy

Write this:
"I will consider selling this stock if ______________."
Examples:

- Revenue declines 3 quarters in a row
- Stock exceeds 100% return in 1 year
- Valuation doubles its fair value
- Company enters legal trouble

This becomes your rational anchor when emotions kick in.

Avoid "All or Nothing" Thinking

You don't need to sell 100% of a stock.
You can:

- Trim a portion
- Take out your original capital
- Rebalance slowly

Think in layers, not in absolutes.

Journal Your Exit

After selling:

- Record why you exited
- How you feel
- What you learned

Over time, these entries will help you see patterns—and improve judgment.

Regret-Proof Your Exits

Here's the truth:
You *will* sell too early sometimes. You *will* hold too long sometimes. You *will* miss a few rallies.
But if your decisions were:

- Thoughtful
- Aligned with your strategy
- Made without panic

Then you haven't failed.
You've matured.
Because in this game, the goal isn't perfection—it's preservation and progress.

Final Analogy: The House You Once Loved

Think of your stocks like real estate.
You buy a house. It serves you well. But one day, the area changes. Crime rises. Schools weaken. Water is an issue.

You don't panic. You assess. And then—you sell.
Not because the house wasn't once right. But because it's no longer aligned with your life.
Your stocks are no different.
You don't owe eternal loyalty to your portfolio. You owe loyalty to your future.

One-Line Summary

Selling isn't weakness—it's wisdom, when done with clarity. Know your reasons. Trust your process. Exit without guilt. Or stay with conviction.

Chapter 18: Losing Is Also a Move

How to lose gracefully, learn, and realign your approach.

Let's start with a sentence no one likes hearing:

You will lose money in the market.

At some point. In some stock. Maybe small. Maybe large. But it will happen.

Not because you're reckless. Not because you're unlucky. But because this is part of the game.

And guess what?

That's okay.

In fact, it's more than okay.

Losing—if handled well—is one of the most important moves you'll ever make.

Because how you react to loss determines whether you grow or just grieve.

This chapter is about learning to lose gracefully, analyze wisely, and return stronger.

The Psychology of a Loss

Let's unpack why losing feels so devastating—especially in investing.

1. It Feels Like a Personal Failure

You picked the stock. You made the call. It dropped. Now it feels like *you* failed—not just the investment.

But that's not true.

Every investor loses sometimes. Even the best. Especially the best.

Warren Buffett lost billions on Kraft Heinz. Ray Dalio misread entire cycles. Howard Marks got crushed in downturns.

The difference? They didn't panic—they processed.

2. We're Not Taught to Accept Loss

School rewards right answers. Jobs reward performance. Markets? They reward resilience.

No one teaches us to lose well.

But in investing, losing is not optional—only your response is.

3. It Hurts More Than It Should

Behavioral economists call this "loss aversion."

Losing ₹10,000 hurts twice as much as gaining ₹10,000 feels good.

This makes us:

- Panic-sell
- Over-correct
- Avoid risk altogether

The result? Fear-driven portfolios that miss long-term upside.

The Reframe: Loss as Tuition

What if you stopped calling it a *loss*—and started calling it a lesson?

Think of it as tuition.

You paid to learn:

- That hype isn't strategy

- That short-term timing rarely works
- That diversification protects
- That emotions cloud logic
- That research matters

A ₹5,000 loss that saves you from a ₹50,000 mistake later? That's a discount.

Every scar becomes structure.

Losses shape:

- Your filters
- Your patience
- Your strategy
- Your humility

They teach things no bull market ever will.

The Art of Losing Well

Let's learn how to lose like a player, not a panicker.

1. Acknowledge It Without Drama

Say it aloud:

"This didn't work out. And that's part of the process."

No shame. No excuses. No denial.

Naming it reduces its power over you.

2. Review the Timeline, Not Just the Outcome

Don't just look at the result. Study:

- Why you entered
- What you expected

- What actually happened
- When it went off-track

Sometimes the company changed. Sometimes your reasoning was off. Sometimes... it was just market chaos.

If you understand *why* you lost—you upgrade your next decision.

3. Write a "Loss Log"

Document every meaningful loss in a journal:

Date	Stock	Reason for Entry	What Went Wrong	What I Learned
Jan 2023	XYZ Ltd.	Fast growth, social buzz	No profits, poor management	Don't buy hype—check earnings

This becomes your personal textbook—written in real money.

4. Avoid the Revenge Trade

This is crucial.

Many investors, after a loss, try to "win it back" quickly:

- Riskier bets
- Bigger positions
- Emotional trades

This is how small mistakes become financial fires.

Don't seek revenge. Seek realignment.

After a loss, pause. Review. Rebuild.

The Math of Losing (And Recovering)

Let's break the illusion of "just bouncing back."

% Loss	% Gain Required to Recover
10%	11.1%
20%	25%
30%	43%
50%	100%

The deeper the loss, the harder the climb.
That's why learning to cut losses—or avoid them early—is key.
But it also means: Don't let ego trap you. If something's clearly wrong—exit.

Learn, Realign, Re-enter

A great player doesn't just lose and mope. They lose, reflect, and reframe their game.
Here's how to bounce back wisely.

Step 1: Reassess Your Filters

- Did you rush the decision?
- Did you trust a tip instead of your own reasoning?
- Did you ignore red flags?

Use the loss to upgrade your selection process.

Step 2: Redefine Your Risk Limits

- Set stop-loss percentages

- Cap exposure to one sector or stock
- Define exit triggers in advance

A player protects their downside before chasing upside.

Step 3: Reconnect With Your Philosophy

Losses shake us. They make us question everything.
So revisit:

- Why you invest
- Your timeline
- Your bigger goal

Let your long view correct your short-term wobble.

Step 4: Rebuild Slowly

Don't rush back in.
Start small:

- With higher conviction
- With clarity
- With balance

The best comeback isn't dramatic—it's disciplined.

The Mental Shift: Losing Without Losing Yourself

The worst loss isn't financial. It's when you lose:

- Your confidence

- Your conviction
- Your belief in the game

That's what you must guard most.

Your job is not to be right every time.

Your job is to:

- Play consistently
- Think clearly
- Improve steadily

The market will humble you. But it can also sharpen you—if you don't run.
A loser who learns becomes a leader.

Final Analogy: The Chessboard of Investing

In chess, even grandmasters lose pieces.
They sacrifice. They adapt. They lose small to win big.
What matters isn't each piece. It's the position, the pattern, and the endgame.
Investing is no different.
You will lose a few stocks. But your position—the strength of your mindset, philosophy, and behavior—can still win the game.

One-Line Summary

Losing is not the opposite of winning. It's one of the moves that teaches you how *to win.*

Chapter 19: Your Game Is Not Their Game

Ignore noise. Build your unique strategy.

You're scrolling through your feed. A friend posts a chart—"100% returns in 6 months." A YouTuber says, "Only fools hold for decades. Here's what I'm buying." A tweet goes viral: *"If you're not doing X with your money, you're being left behind."*

You feel something shift.

Not in your portfolio—but in your mind.

You start doubting your own plan. You feel behind. You feel small. You wonder: *"Am I missing something?"*

Welcome to the comparison trap.

In this chapter, we'll break it.

Because your investing journey is not a group project. It's not a competition. And it's definitely not a race.

Your game is not their game. And the moment you forget that, you start losing—not money, but clarity.

Let's learn to build a strategy that's yours, not borrowed. Aligned, not influenced. And most importantly—respected by you, not just others.

The World Is Loud. Your Plan Must Be Quiet.

Let's be honest—this era of investing is louder than ever.

You're bombarded with:

- Portfolio screenshots
- 15-second "tips"
- Overnight success stories
- Hot takes from strangers
- "I told you so" threads
- Viral panic during every dip

You're surrounded by opinions pretending to be facts, and results pretending to be repeatable.
And if you're not careful, this noise can:

- Hijack your focus
- Rewrite your goals
- Push you into decisions that feel right—but aren't right for you

Everyone seems to be winning online. But what they're playing for—and how they're playing—might be nothing like your game.

Why We Compare (And Why It's So Dangerous)

1. Social Proof Feels Like Safety
You see 100 people buying a certain stock. It feels validated. Safe. Proven.
But crowd behavior is not strategy. It's emotion—multiplied.
2. We Mistake Visibility for Wisdom
Just because someone's loud or popular doesn't mean they're right.
Virality ≠ credibility. Certainty ≠ accuracy.
3. We Internalize Other People's Goals

He's trading for fast cash. She's investing for early retirement. They're gambling. You're building for 20 years.
But now you're thinking, *"Should I be doing what they're doing?"*
This is how strategies collapse. When you borrow someone's moves—but not their context.

The Cost of Playing Someone Else's Game

Let's play this out.

Scenario 1: You copy a trader

- They flip stocks weekly.
- You try the same.
- But you don't have the time, tools, or tolerance.
- You lose money—and confidence.

Scenario 2: You mimic a long-term investor

- But your real goal was a 3-year home fund.
- Now your money is stuck.
- You feel frustrated—and confused.

Scenario 3: You follow a friend's tip

- They win. You lose.
- You question yourself.
- You either blame the market—or give up.

All of this happens because you forgot:
They're playing their game. You're living your life.

Reclaiming Your Game: The 5 Questions That Rebuild Clarity

Let's return to your side of the table.

These five questions will center you.

1. What Is My Money For?

Be specific:

- Retirement?
- Buying a house?
- Gaining freedom from a job?
- Funding a child's education?

Your goal defines your:

- Time horizon
- Risk appetite
- Portfolio design

If you don't define your finish line, you'll keep running other people's races.

2. What Kind of Risk Am I Comfortable With?

Are you:

- Cool with volatility?
- Okay seeing red for months if long-term upside is big?
- More conservative by nature?

Your comfort determines:

- Stock selection
- Allocation

- Holding behavior

If you copy someone who can emotionally tolerate -40% dips—but you can't—you'll always exit at the worst time.

3. What Is My Time Commitment?

Do you:

- Have hours to analyze charts and news?
- Or just 1 hour a month to review?

Your availability shapes your style.

Don't borrow strategies from full-time traders if you're a part-time investor.

4. Do I Enjoy This—or Just Endure It?

Some people love charts. Some people love reading annual reports. Others prefer simplicity—automated index funds, SIPs, passive growth.

There's no one right way.

But there is a wrong way: forcing yourself into a strategy you hate.

Sustainability matters more than sophistication.

5. What Will Let Me Sleep at Night?

That's your real benchmark.

- Is it balance?
- Stability?
- Growth with calm?
- Or chasing speed?

If you can't sleep when a stock dips 10%, your portfolio isn't built around you.

It's built around someone else's comfort—and that's a recipe for regret.

Signs That You're Finally Playing Your Own Game

- You don't chase tips
- You don't panic during noise
- You don't envy others' returns
- You don't explain your every move
- You feel at peace—even when you're holding steady

That's real power.
That's an investor—not a follower.

Build a Strategy That Looks Like You

Let's put it into action.

Step 1: Choose Your Investment Style

- Passive Index Investing?
- Long-Term Equity Picking?
- Dividends?
- Value?
- Sector-focused?
- A blended mix?

Don't chase complexity. Choose clarity.

Step 2: Set Your Allocation Framework

For example:

- 60% stable long-term holdings
- 20% aggressive high-growth bets
- 10% cash buffer
- 10% experimental ideas or ETFs

Customize it. Make it *yours*.

Step 3: Define Your Review Rhythm

- Monthly?
- Quarterly?
- Annually?

Avoid daily stress. Build confidence through rhythm.

Step 4: Write Your Strategy Statement

"I invest for long-term freedom through simple, high-conviction companies. I'm okay missing short-term gains for peace of mind. I'll review every quarter, stay diversified, and only invest what I understand."
Print it. Read it. Live by it.

Silencing the Noise (Without Hating the World)

You don't have to isolate yourself. Just insulate your thinking. How?

- Mute hype accounts

- Follow people who teach, not preach
- Filter information through your plan
- Don't engage in performance comparisons
- Celebrate your calm—not just your returns

The moment you stop needing to impress others, you start building something real.

Final Analogy: The Playground vs. the Chessboard

Most investors act like kids on a noisy playground:

- Everyone running
- Shouting
- Mimicking each other
- Not sure what the game even is

But you?
You're sitting at a quiet chessboard.
You move with intent. You hold your posture. You're not rushed.
Because you're not here to win their games. You're here to master your own.

One-Line Summary

The market has many players—but only one portfolio that matters: yours. Build it around your life, *not their noise.*

Interlude

You Stayed. That's the Real Win.

Because survival is underrated—and endurance is everything.

You've come a long way—not just as an investor, but as a person.

You've built more than a portfolio. You've built posture. Patience. Perspective.

Level 4 wasn't about buying or selling. It wasn't about timing or tactics. It was about learning how not to quit.

And that? That's rare.

Most people leave the game when:

- The screen turns red
- The media screams panic
- Their expectations aren't met
- Someone else seems to be doing "better"

But you?

You learned to sit still. To wait. To think. To breathe. To not check your portfolio every 10 minutes. To lose—without losing yourself.

You didn't flinch at every wave. You understood the tide. You didn't chase every tip. You returned to your plan. You didn't try to be perfect. You tried to stay present.

And that's what separates players from pretenders.

Now, you're ready for the final level—not just winning more money, but winning more meaning.

Because beyond the charts, the tools, and the terms... The real game is about who you become while you play.

Level 5: Next Stages

Chapter 20: Beyond Stocks

Funds, ETFs, and Other Leagues

The simplified world of passive investing and global diversification.

Up to this point, we've focused mostly on stocks—individual companies, investor behavior, personal strategy.

But here's the truth:

You don't need to handpick every stock to be a successful investor.

You don't need to analyze balance sheets late into the night.

You don't need to chase the next big winner.

In fact, there's a quieter, simpler, and incredibly effective path that many smart investors take—especially those who:

- Don't want to spend hours each month studying the market
- Prefer stability over thrill
- Want global exposure with minimal complexity
- Are playing a long, steady game

This chapter is about that path.

Welcome to the world of passive investing: ETFs. Index funds. Mutual funds. Global baskets. Sectoral exposures.

You're still in the game—just playing in a league that values consistency over chaos.

Let's break it down, with zero jargon and maximum clarity.

The Problem With Picking Stocks for Everyone

Individual stocks are great for:

- Deep learners
- Active investors
- Sector specialists
- People who enjoy analysis and volatility

But let's face it:

- Not everyone enjoys that
- Not everyone has time
- And not every market is easy to understand

That's where funds come in.
Think of them as:
"Ready-made portfolios" crafted to give you exposure, diversification, and strategy—without you needing to micro-manage."

Mutual Funds, Index Funds & ETFs – What's the Difference?

Let's simplify the three most popular vehicles.

1. Mutual Funds

- Actively managed by fund managers
- Pool of investor money invested into a basket of

stocks, bonds, or other assets
- Higher fees due to active management
- Often comes with SIP (Systematic Investment Plan) options

Use Case: Great for beginners who want a professional to manage selection and timing.

2. Index Funds

- A type of mutual fund
- Passively tracks a specific market index (like Nifty 50, S&P 500)
- Lower cost than actively managed mutual funds
- No human judgment—just follows the index composition

Use Case: Ideal for long-term investors who want market-average returns with minimal costs.

3. ETFs (Exchange-Traded Funds)

- Similar to index funds—but traded on stock exchanges like individual stocks
- Prices fluctuate during the trading day
- Very low cost
- Offers easy diversification—across markets, sectors, countries

Use Case: Great for those who want flexibility, transparency, and global access.

Key Differences Summary:

Feature	Mutual Funds	Index Funds	ETFs
Management	Active	Passive	Passive
Costs	Medium–High	Low	Very Low
Liquidity	End-of-day NAV	End-of-day NAV	Real-time trading
Flexibility	Fixed SIPs	Fixed SIPs	Buy/sell anytime
Transparency	Medium	High	Very High

Why You Should Consider Diversification Beyond Domestic Stocks

If your entire portfolio is built around:

- Indian stocks (or only U.S. stocks)
- One sector (tech, pharma, etc.)
- One currency (INR, USD)

Then you're exposed to local risk—currency, politics, inflation, economic cycles.
Smart investors don't put all their eggs in one economy.
Global ETFs and mutual funds give you access to:

- U.S. tech giants (Google, Apple, Microsoft)
- Emerging markets (Brazil, Vietnam, South Africa)
- European blue-chips
- Thematic trends (green energy, AI, cybersecurity)

Geographical diversification is no longer a luxury—it's a survival strategy in a global economy.

Passive Investing: What It Means (And Why It Works)

"Passive" doesn't mean lazy. It means strategically choosing to play a different game.

Active vs. Passive:

Approach	Active	Passive
Objective	Beat the market	Match the market
Effort	High	Low
Costs	Higher fees	Lower fees
Outcome	High variance	Stable performance
Ideal For	Traders, enthusiasts	Long-term builders

Why Passive Investing Wins for Most People:

- 80–90% of actively managed funds fail to beat their benchmarks over 10+ years
- Passive funds have lower fees, meaning more money stays invested
- You're not trying to time the market—you're riding with it
- It's emotion-proof—no panic, no chasing hype

Passive investing is how you build wealth while living your life.

Building a Simple Passive Portfolio (Example)

Let's say you want a passive, globally diversified portfolio.

Here's a sample mix:

Asset Class	Instrument	Allocation
Domestic Market	Nifty 50 Index Fund / ETF	30%
Global Exposure	S&P 500 ETF / Nasdaq ETF	30%
Emerging Markets	EM ETF / International Mutual Fund	10%
Bonds / Debt	Debt Mutual Fund / Gilt Fund	20%
Gold / Hedge	Gold ETF / Sovereign Gold Bonds	10%

You can automate this monthly via SIPs—or review quarterly. This portfolio needs 30 minutes a quarter to manage. It gives you access to thousands of companies across the globe—without stock-picking stress.

Common Passive Investing Products (India & Global)

India:

- **Index Funds**: HDFC Nifty 50, UTI Nifty Next 50, ICICI Sensex Fund
- **ETFs**: Nippon India Nifty Bees, Motilal Oswal Nasdaq 100 ETF, Mirae Asset S&P 500 ETF
- **Debt Funds**: SBI Gilt Fund, Bharat Bond ETF
- **Gold ETFs**: HDFC Gold ETF, SGBs (Sovereign Gold Bonds)

Global (for U.S. investors or global platforms):

- VOO: Vanguard S&P 500 ETF
- QQQ: Nasdaq 100 ETF
- VT: Vanguard Total World Stock ETF
- ARKK: ARK Innovation ETF (for thematic exposure)
- BND: Total Bond Market ETF

When Passive Is the Best Active Decision

You might say:
"Isn't picking passive products also a decision?"
Yes—and that's the beauty.
You make a few big decisions that protect you from hundreds of small, reactive ones.

- You choose simplicity over prediction
- You choose systems over heroics
- You choose probability over popularity

And in doing so, you opt out of the stress game while still compounding wealth.

What Passive Investing Is Not

- It's not giving up control.
- It's not underperforming.
- It's not boring—it's boring on purpose.

The goal isn't to impress. It's to endure.

You'll never see a passive investor going viral. But you'll see them quietly build wealth while others burn out.

Final Analogy: The Elevator vs. the Staircase

Picking individual stocks is like running up the stairs—fast, risky, and tiring. Sometimes you reach faster. Sometimes you fall.

Passive investing is like taking the elevator:

- It's slower to start
- It's steady
- But it gets you there—with less effort, fewer errors, and far more peace

And in the long run, peace *compounds*, too.

One-Line Summary

You don't need to chase brilliance. Sometimes, letting the world work for you—through funds and ETFs—is the smartest move you'll ever make.

Chapter 21: The Future of the Game

AI, Algorithms, and Human Intuition

Where markets are headed and how to stay relevant.

Let's fast forward.

The year is 2035. An AI assistant opens your investment dashboard and says:

"Would you like me to reallocate based on real-time market stress patterns and your updated sleep data?"

Strange? Not really.

Because even today:

- Trades are executed in microseconds by machines.
- Stock advice is generated by large language models.
- Retail investors follow AI-curated portfolios.
- Entire markets move based on algorithmic triggers.

The future of investing is already here. It's automated, accelerated, and almost alien—but you still have a place in it.

This chapter explores that evolving future. It helps you understand where the game is headed, and how to remain not just present—but powerful.

Let's explore what changes. And what doesn't.

The Rise of AI and Algorithmic Trading

Let's break it down.

What is Algorithmic Trading?

Also called "algo trading" or "quant trading," it refers to:

- Automated systems that buy/sell securities based on pre-set rules
- Execution based on technical indicators, news flow, or arbitrage opportunities
- Speed, scale, and logic that no human can match

More than 70% of global trading volume today is algorithmic. These bots:

- React faster than headlines can break
- Trade without emotion
- Spot price inefficiencies in milliseconds
- Dominate short-term momentum

What About AI?

AI is now:

- Predicting earnings outcomes
- Analyzing sentiment from news and social media
- Generating asset allocation models based on risk profiles
- Powering robo-advisors that manage entire portfolios
- Learning your behavior to optimize investing decisions

And it's only just beginning.
Soon, AI could:

- Create hyper-personalized strategies in real-time
- Warn you before you make a bad trade
- Adjust your portfolio automatically during global events
- Integrate with wearables to assess your stress tolerance

The investor of tomorrow may look more like a *curator of models* than a picker of stocks.

Should You Be Worried? Or Excited?

Let's be honest. It's both.
AI is not just a tool. It's a force multiplier. It's changing:

- Speed – markets move faster
- Scale – anyone can now invest globally
- Access – insights that were elite are now free
- Expectations – everyone wants "smart portfolios" instantly

But here's the twist:
The human investor still matters—just not in the old way.
Your edge isn't speed anymore. It's not raw data access. It's not even instinctive prediction.
Your new edge is:

- Interpretation
- Values
- Emotional discipline
- Philosophy
- Perspective

The machine may pick stocks. But you still pick meaning.

What AI Can't Do (Yet—and Maybe Never)

Let's clarify what the bots can't replace:

1. Purpose-Based Investing

AI can optimize for returns. But it can't decide *why* you're investing.

Only you can connect investing to:

- Freedom
- Family
- Impact
- Peace of mind
- Legacy

Machines trade money. Humans build lives.

2. Long-Term Emotional Navigation

AI doesn't panic. You do. And that's where your self-awareness matters most.

You must learn to:

- Sit through uncertainty
- Resist FOMO
- Stick to your timeline
- Say no to speed for the sake of stability

The future investor needs emotional algorithms as much as financial ones.

3. Ethical Alignment

AI doesn't care where returns come from. But you might.

You may want to avoid:

- Weapon manufacturers
- Tobacco companies
- Data-mining social platforms
- Fossil fuel giants

Your portfolio reflects your values, not just your goals.
That part remains deeply human.

The Hybrid Future: AI + You

So how do we thrive in this new landscape?
By not competing against machines—but evolving with them.
Here's how.

1. Use AI as a Filter, Not a Final Word

Let AI help you:

- Screen stocks
- Summarize reports
- Map historical data
- Identify anomalies

But make the final decision with your values and goals in mind.

2. Create a Human-Machine Framework

Here's an example:

- AI suggests a portfolio based on volatility tolerance
- You edit it based on your life timeline and priorities
- AI rebalances it quarterly
- You reflect annually on your real-life progress

It's not about control. It's about co-creation.

3. Automate the Routine—Stay Human in the Big Picture

Automate:

- SIPs
- Rebalancing thresholds
- Tax harvesting

But stay involved in:

- Asset allocation strategy
- Portfolio philosophy
- Life alignment reviews

The machine executes. You evolve.

How to Future-Proof Your Strategy

Let's make this practical.

To remain relevant, do these three things:

1. Master Your Philosophy, Not Just Your Tools

Technology will keep changing. But your investment philosophy should stay steady.

Revisit:

- What do I stand for financially?
- What kind of investor am I?
- What matters more—freedom or fame, peace or performance?

The more the market automates, the more you must self-define.

2. Learn "Enough" to Converse Intelligently
You don't need to become a coder. But understand:

- What an ETF really does
- What your robo-advisor is optimizing for
- The difference between smart beta and classic indexing

Financial literacy is your shield in an AI-first world.
3. Stay Flexible, Curious, and Calm
The investor of the future is:

- Not rigid
- Not obsessed with being right
- Not threatened by change

They're adaptable.
They think:
"If the game evolves, so will I."
And that mindset? It's timeless.

Final Analogy: The Compass and the Autopilot

Imagine flying a plane with autopilot.
The machine can:

- Control altitude
- Adjust for wind
- Monitor systems

But you still need a destination. You still need to course-correct in storms. You still need to land the plane.

AI is your autopilot. Your philosophy is the compass. Your awareness is the pilot's instinct.

Don't give up the cockpit. Share it—with intention.

One-Line Summary

The future of investing is fast, smart, and automated—but your clarity, purpose, and emotional wisdom will always be the real edge.

Chapter 22: Final Word

Win Without Winning

The real goal isn't beating others. It's aligning your money with your mind.

There's a strange silence that follows financial success.

You grow your portfolio. You hit the number you once dreamed of. You beat the index. You bought the dips. You held through fear. You stayed the course.

And yet... something feels incomplete.

Because all along, you thought *winning the market* would make you feel like you'd won at life.

But it doesn't—unless your external progress was always aligned with your internal purpose.

The truth is, you can beat the market and still feel lost. And you can trail behind and still feel whole—if your money, mind, and meaning are in sync.

This final chapter is not about numbers. It's about something quieter and far more powerful.

Let's redefine what it means to *win without winning.*

What Most People Think "Winning" Is

- Picking the best stocks
- Timing the perfect exit
- Beating your friends' returns

- Retiring early with a fat portfolio
- Predicting the crash before everyone else
- Showing off screenshots and CAGR

That's what the world celebrates.
It's loud. Flashy. Often temporary.
But true wealth? It's what the world doesn't see.
Let's explore that.

What Real Winning Feels Like

1. Calm in Uncertainty
You're not shaken by every red screen. You don't flinch at headlines. You trust your process.
You're emotionally free.
2. Clarity of Purpose
You know *why* you invest. It's not just money—it's meaning. Your wealth is directed, not drifting.
You're intentional, not reactive.
3. Freedom from Comparison
You don't care what someone else is holding. You don't chase viral stocks. You're not running anyone's race.
You've built your own game—and stayed in it.
4. Your Life Is Funded by Peace, Not Pressure
You sleep well. You take breaks without guilt. Your money supports your life—not the other way around.
Your net worth doesn't determine your self-worth.
5. You're Still Curious—But Not Compulsive
You read, learn, listen. But you're not always chasing. You can observe the market without being consumed by it.
You're guided by rhythm, not urgency.

Because Money Isn't the Game—It's the Tool

Somewhere along the way, we started thinking that investing was about money as the finish line.
It's not.
Money is:

- A medium
- A tool
- A multiplier
- A messenger
- A mirror

It shows you:

- How patient you are
- How impulsive you are
- How clear you are
- How greedy, scared, or grounded you are

But it's not *you.*
You are the one playing this game. And the goal was never to just collect chips. It was to learn how to move—with wisdom, peace, and clarity.

Winning Without Winning Means...

1. You Can Lose and Still Be Proud
You held through a loss. You didn't blame. You reflected. You adapted.
That's emotional maturity. That's a win.
2. You Can Miss Out—and Still Sleep Well

You didn't buy the hot IPO. You didn't double your money like your cousin. But you stayed true to your plan.
That's integrity. That's a win.

3. You Can Have Less—but Need Less, Too

You didn't chase a bigger portfolio at the cost of your health, peace, or presence.
That's alignment. That's a win.

4. You Can Make Others Feel Safe With Money

You taught your kids not to fear the market. You helped a friend invest calmly. You shared knowledge instead of secrets.
That's contribution. That's a win.

5. You Become the Kind of Person Who Doesn't Need To Win

You enjoy the game without obsessing over scoreboards. You invest without over-identifying. You grow without performing.
That's liberation. That's the ultimate win.

Rewrite Your Scoreboard

Let's throw away the leaderboard that everyone uses.
Replace it with something real.
Create your own personal performance dashboard:

Metric	True Investor's Benchmark
Peace	"I don't panic in volatility."
Clarity	"I know why I hold what I hold."
Consistency	"I follow my plan, not my mood."
Generosity	"I teach others or share what I learn."
Freedom	"I use money to live, not to prove."
Awareness	"I reflect before I react."

Let this be your new scoreboard.

Because that's what will matter 10, 20, 30 years from now.
Not who won the dip-buy. But who remained true to themselves while growing.

Final Analogy: The Infinite Game

In *finite games*, there are winners and losers. There's a clear end. A trophy. A final score.
But investing isn't like that.
Investing is an infinite game.
The point is not to win—but to keep playing:

- Through life changes
- Through market cycles
- Through evolving goals
- Through lessons and losses

And the only way to keep playing is to keep learning—and to stay whole.

A Quiet Victory

If you close this book:

- With more confidence
- With more calm
- With more curiosity
- With more clarity
- With more courage

Then you've already won.

Even if your portfolio is down 2%. Even if you didn't "crack the code." Even if your progress is slow.

Because you're no longer just reacting. You're now responding.

And that, dear reader, is the true transformation.

One-Line Summary

Winning in the market isn't about being first, fastest, or famous—it's about being free, focused, and fully aligned with who you are.

This is the end of the book—but the beginning of your game.

Closing Note

Stay in the Game. But Stay Yourself.

If you've made it this far, thank you—for reading, reflecting, and most importantly, choosing to be a more intentional player in this strange, beautiful game called the market.

You now know more than many who have been in the game for years. But what will set you apart isn't your stock picks or your returns It's your awareness.

You'll face noise. You'll miss opportunities. You'll doubt yourself. You'll see others move faster, louder, and flashier.

Let them.

You're not here to impress anyone. You're here to grow—with calm, with purpose, and with patience.

You don't need to time the market. You need to trust your rhythm. You don't need to predict the future. You need to align with your values.

Because in the end, the goal isn't to be the richest person in the room. It's to be the one who played with peace, clarity, and no regrets.

So stay curious. Stay honest. Stay in the game. But above all—stay yourself.

The market will change. Your life will change. But your clarity? That's your real wealth.

See you on the field.

— *Sandeep*

Appendices

Appendix A: Game Glossary

Speak the Market Language Without Sounding Like a Trader

Investing can feel like walking into a room where everyone is speaking a secret language—buzzwords flying around, charts blinking, voices echoing phrases like "bullish breakout" and "overbought RSI."

Let's decode that room.

This glossary isn't about impressing anyone with jargon. It's about **understanding what actually matters**—so you can hold your ground, ask better questions, and never feel out of place again.

Share / Stock / Equity:

Different names, same idea: a piece of ownership in a company. When you buy a stock, you own a small part of that business—its profits, its risks, and its future.

Market

A space—physical or digital—where people buy and sell shares. Think of it as the world's busiest supermarket, except the shelves are lined with companies instead of groceries.

Portfolio

Your personal basket of investments. It could include stocks, funds, bonds, gold, etc. Like your wardrobe, it reflects your style, priorities, and sometimes... your regrets.

Dividend

A payout a company gives you from its profits—like a thank-you note, but with money.

Index

A collection of stocks designed to represent a portion of the market (e.g., Nifty 50, S&P 500). Think of it like a scoreboard—it shows how a segment of the market is doing.

Mutual Fund

A pooled fund managed by a professional. You and others invest together, and a fund manager decides where the money goes. Great for passive investors who want diversification with less direct involvement.

ETF (Exchange-Traded Fund)

Like a mutual fund, but it trades like a stock. Low cost, real-time flexibility, and usually tracks an index or theme.

Bull Market

When the market rises confidently over time. Optimism is high. Everyone suddenly becomes a financial genius.

Bear Market

When the market falls significantly, usually 20% or more from recent highs. Pessimism reigns. Even your dog stops checking stock prices.

Valuation

What a company is "worth" in market terms. Different from price. Valuation reflects a deeper assessment—like a house appraisal, not just its sale tag.

Fundamentals

The real stuff: revenue, profit, debt, management, business model. Think of it as the engine under the hood.

Technical Analysis

Using charts and patterns to predict price movements. Popular among traders, often dismissed by long-term investors. It's the "weather forecast" of the market.

Fundamental Analysis

Looking at the company's actual performance and potential to assess value. This is the slow cooker of investing—takes time, but delivers depth.

Rebalancing

Adjusting your portfolio to stay in line with your original goals. If one stock or fund has grown too big, you trim it and spread things back into balance. Like trimming a bonsai tree.

Capital Gain

Profit earned from selling a stock or asset at a higher price than you bought it for. Taxable, but very satisfying.

SIP (Systematic Investment Plan)

A fixed-amount investment done periodically (usually monthly) in a fund. Like setting up a fitness plan for your money.

Asset Allocation

How you divide your money among different asset classes (stocks, bonds, gold, etc.). It's your strategy map—and the most important part of your financial GPS.

Volatility

How fast and unpredictably prices move. High volatility = more drama. Not always bad, just more emotional.

Risk Tolerance

How much loss you can emotionally and financially absorb. Everyone says they have high risk tolerance—until the first red screen.

Correction

A market drop of 10% or more. Not a crash—more like a timeout. Often a healthy reset.

Stop-Loss

A trigger point to sell a stock if it drops to a certain level, to limit potential loss. Like airbags for your trades.

Speculation

Investing based more on hope, hype, or trends than research. Sometimes works. Often doesn't. Handle with caution.

Compounding

The snowball effect: your money earns returns, and those returns earn returns. Over time, it becomes magical. Time is the multiplier.

Patience

Not a market term, but the most underrated one in this book. The real compounding engine lives in your ability to wait.

Final Thought:

This glossary is not a dictionary—it's a toolkit. Use what's useful. Forget what's flashy. And remember, **you don't need to sound like a trader to think like an investor.**

Appendix B: Portfolio Blueprint Template

Build from Zero

A simple, guided framework to go from blank slate to confident investor.
Let's face it—most people never build a portfolio because they feel they're missing:

- The time
- The knowledge
- The perfect market moment
- The magic first stock

But here's the truth:
You don't need to be an expert. You just need a plan that fits **you.**
This blueprint is designed to help you build that plan. Step by step. With calm. Without fear. And absolutely no pressure to be brilliant.
Let's build your portfolio like a player—not a follower.

Step 1: Define Your Financial Intentions

Before picking anything, ask:

1. What is this money for?

- Retirement
- A house
- Financial freedom
- Education
- Security
- Legacy

2. What is my time horizon?
    - Short (1–3 years)
    - Medium (3–7 years)
    - Long (7+ years)
3. How much emotional risk can I handle?
    - I panic easily
    - I'm okay with fluctuations
    - I ignore the news and sleep like a monk

Your answers here will shape every choice ahead.

Step 2: Choose Your Strategy Style

Pick a base approach:

Style	Description	Good for
Passive	Index funds, ETFs, low involvement	Peace-seekers, beginners
Hybrid	Mix of index funds + a few handpicked stocks	Curious learners
Active	Individual stock picking, sector plays	Research lovers, market watchers

There's no perfect choice. Just what fits your personality and life rhythm.

Step 3: Your Ideal Allocation Mix

A suggested starting point (can be adjusted based on your age, goals, and risk tolerance):

Asset Class	Purpose	Suggested Allocation
Domestic Equity (Index Funds / Stocks)	Growth & wealth building	40–60%
Global Equity (ETFs / International Funds)	Diversification & currency hedge	10–30%
Debt / Bonds / Gilt Funds	Stability & income	10–25%
Gold / Commodities	Inflation protection & hedge	5–10%
Cash / Liquid Funds	Flexibility & emergencies	5–10%

You can start small in each category—even ₹500 per month per fund.

Step 4: Choose Your Investment Rhythm

Your action plan:

- Automate SIPs (Systematic Investment Plans) monthly
- Set quarterly portfolio check-ins
- Review allocation once per year
- Avoid daily tracking unless you're actively trading

Compounding doesn't need your micromanagement—it needs your consistency.

Step 5: Pick Sample Instruments (India + Global)

Here's a sample list to guide beginners. Always check fees, track record, and your platform access.

Goal	Type	Sample Option
Domestic Equity	Nifty 50 / Sensex Index Fund	UTI Nifty Index Fund, HDFC Sensex Fund
Global Equity	U.S. Tech Exposure	Motilal Oswal Nasdaq 100 ETF
Bonds / Debt	Safety & stability	SBI Gilt Fund, Bharat Bond ETF
Gold	Inflation hedge	HDFC Gold ETF, Sovereign Gold Bonds
Cash Reserve	Flexibility	ICICI Liquid Fund, Axis Overnight Fund

Adjust based on your location, currency, and broker platform.

Step 6: Track Like a Player (Not a Perfectionist)

Use this simple tracker once a quarter:

Asset / Fund	Holding	Allocation %	Return	Feeling About It?
Nifty Index Fund	₹X,XXX	40%	+7%	Still aligned
Gold ETF	₹X,XXX	10%	-1%	Holding
U.S. ETF	₹X,XXX	20%	+12%	Might increase

Note: "Feeling About It?" is not a joke—your **emotional alignment** matters as much as returns.

Step 7: Review Triggers (When to Make Changes)

You don't need to "do something" all the time. But have a few predefined triggers:

- 3 consecutive quarters of underperformance → Review, not panic
- Goal milestone hit → Consider partial exit
- Allocation drifts by 15–20% → Rebalance
- Life change (job loss, child, move) → Reassess overall plan

Let rules guide you. Not moods.

Final Encouragement

This template isn't about perfection. It's about **traction**. And your first ₹500 investment is more powerful than a thousand pages of hesitation.

Keep it simple. Keep it aligned. Keep showing up.

Your best portfolio won't be the one that's most exciting. It will be the one that **quietly works**, while you live a meaningful life.

Appendix C: Reflective Investor Journal Template

A simple tool to track your thoughts, not just your returns.

Most investors track numbers. Very few track decisions. Almost none track emotions.

And yet—it's your thoughts and feelings, not your brokerage dashboard, that determine how well you actually perform over time.

This isn't just about data. It's about depth. It's about learning from your own behavior—so you can evolve from a participant to a **player with perspective**.

Use this journal monthly, quarterly, or after every meaningful investing action. It's not for anyone else. It's for **you**—to slow down, reflect, and get better.

Let's build the muscle that matters most: **your self-awareness.**

Section 1: My Investing Snapshot (Date: ___________)

Prompt	Your Notes
What did I buy, sell, or review recently?	
What was my reasoning at the time?	
Was it based on data, instinct, influence, or emotion?	
How do I feel about it today? (Excited, anxious, neutral?)	

Section 2: Strategy Check-In

Prompt	Your Notes
Is my current portfolio aligned with my original plan?	
Has anything changed in my life that requires a reassessment?	
Am I chasing any stocks or trends out of FOMO or comparison?	
Do I still understand every asset I hold?	
What would I do differently if I were starting fresh today?	

Section 3: Emotional Weather Forecast

Rate yourself from 1–5:

Emotional State	Rating (1 = low, 5 = high)	Notes
Confidence in my portfolio		
Urge to make a big move		
Patience with long-term goals		
Trust in my own judgment		
Noise or anxiety from the market		

A low rating isn't a red flag—it's a signal for reflection.

Section 4: Lessons & Insights

Prompt	Your Notes
What have I learned recently—about the market or myself?	
What mistake did I avoid (or make) and why?	
What emotion do I need to manage better in the future?	
What part of my strategy am I proud of?	
What's one action I'll take this quarter to improve?	

Section 5: My Personal Investing Rules (Update Quarterly)

These are YOUR rules. They will evolve. Start simple. Examples:

- "I won't invest in anything I don't understand."

- "I won't check prices more than once a week."
- "I will never invest based on tips from social media."
- "I'll review my allocation every 6 months."
- "I will hold every stock for at least 1 year unless fundamentals change."

Rule No.	Rule	Am I following it?
1		☑/ ✕
2		☑/ ✕
3		☑/ ✕

Section 6: End-of-Quarter Self-Reflection

Complete this after each quarter:
"This quarter, I was most proud of..." "I made one decision I wish I had handled differently..." "I noticed I was most emotionally triggered when..." "My portfolio feels like a reflection of..." "In the next quarter, I want to feel more..."

Why This Journal Works

Because performance is **not just about price.** It's about how well you:

- Stick to your strategy
- Learn from your actions
- Recognize your triggers
- Adapt with awareness
- Grow beyond numbers

This journal doesn't promise perfect returns. It promises **better reflection**—which leads to **better decisions**, which leads to **sustainable growth.**

The smartest investor isn't the one with the best Excel file. It's the one who knows **why** they do what they do—and learns from it.

Appendix D: Emotional Checklist

Before You Buy or Sell

A decision filter for clarity, not chaos.
The worst trades often don't come from lack of knowledge. They come from:

- Sudden excitement
- FOMO (Fear of Missing Out)
- Panic during a dip
- Impatience during stagnation
- Peer pressure disguised as advice

The emotional investor may look logical on the outside—but inside, they're reacting, not deciding.
That's why this checklist exists. To pause your finger just before that "Buy" or "Sell" click—and ask:
"Am I thinking clearly, or just moving fast?"
Use this short, powerful checklist whenever you're tempted to act. It takes just 3–5 minutes—but can save you **years of regret**.

Before You Buy – Pause and Ask

Question	Answer (Yes / No / Unsure)
Do I clearly understand what this company/fund/asset does?	
Am I buying because of my plan—or because someone else is?	
Have I read at least one report, earnings summary or credible article about it?	
Can I explain in one sentence why I'm buying this—without mentioning hype or hope?	
Would I still buy this if no one else knew I did?	
Am I okay holding this if it drops 20% tomorrow?	
Is this aligned with my overall portfolio (not just a shiny add-on)?	
Do I know when and why I'll consider selling it in the future?	

If you answer "No" or "Unsure" to 3 or more—pause. Re-evaluate. Don't rush.

Top Emotional Red Flags Before Buying

If you catch yourself thinking:

- "Everyone is getting into this—what if I miss out?"
- "I need to catch up with my peers."
- "The price keeps going up, I should just get in now."
- "This YouTuber said it's the next big thing."

- "It's down 40%—must be a bargain!"

STOP. Breathe. Reread your philosophy.
Impulse is **not strategy**.

Before You Sell – Pause and Ask

Question	Answer (Yes / No / Unsure)
Am I selling because my thesis (original reason for buying) has changed?	
Has the company/fund actually underperformed on fundamentals—not just price?	
Am I reacting to fear, not strategy?	
Have I held this long enough to allow it to play out (based on my original plan)?	
Do I need this money for something urgent—or is this just panic?	
If this asset went up 10% next week, would I regret selling it today?	
Am I rebalancing with intent—or just running from red?	
Have I consulted my written rules or investment journal before making this decision?	

If more than 2–3 answers are "No" or "Unsure"—hold for now. Review in 24–48 hours.

Top Emotional Red Flags Before Selling

If you find yourself thinking:

- "I just want to get out."

- "I can't take this red anymore."
- "What if it goes to zero?"
- "It's been flat for months—it's useless."
- "Everyone else sold it—I should too."

These are **fear reactions**, not strategy.
Remember: **you bought it for a reason.** Revisit that reason before you override it with emotion.

Your Pre-Trade Mantra (Say it aloud)

"I am not here to look smart. I am not here to chase others. I am here to build patiently, learn deeply, and grow quietly. If I act now, I do it with intention—not emotion."

Why This Checklist Matters

Because every click counts. And while numbers change daily, your mind carries every decision **for years**.
This checklist won't make you perfect. But it will keep you **present**.
And sometimes, that's the only edge you need.

Appendix E: The 5-Year Letter to My Future Self

A conversation with the investor—and human—you're becoming.

The market will change. The world will shift. So will your income, your priorities, your confidence... and maybe even your goals.

But there's one voice that should never get lost in the noise:

Your own.

This appendix is a time capsule. It's not financial advice. It's not a portfolio tracker. It's a **private letter**—from the investor you are now, to the one you're becoming in five years.

You won't share it with your broker. You won't post it online.

You may not even look at it again until you're ready.

But when you do... you'll remember what truly mattered.

Let's write it.

Instructions: How to Use This Letter

1. Set aside 30–45 minutes in a quiet space. No apps, no distractions.
2. Write slowly, honestly, without trying to sound smart.
3. Store this letter in your journal, email it to yourself, or save it with your investment tracker.
4. Set a reminder to open it **exactly 5 years from today.**

What you write today might just protect you from future panic, overconfidence, or regret.
This is your **anchor**.

The 5-Year Letter to My Future Self

(Use the prompts or write it free-flow.)
Date: [Today's Date]
To: My Future Self (5 years from now)
Subject: Remember why you started.
Dear [Your Name],
As I write this, I don't know where the market will be in 5 years. Maybe it's booming. Maybe it's bleeding. Maybe you've doubled your portfolio—or lost half. Maybe AI is running everything. Or maybe... it's just you, still showing up.
But wherever you are, I hope this letter reminds you of a few simple truths.

Why I Started This Journey

I didn't begin investing to impress anyone. I didn't do it to gamble, win arguments, or chase perfection.
I did it because I wanted:

- [example: freedom from worry]
- [example: a way to grow slowly and steadily]
- [example: to provide better for my future family]
- [example: to stop feeling helpless about money]

These are still true. Don't forget them.

My Core Principles Back Then

Here's what I believed—and I hope you still do:

- Investing is a long game, not a lottery.
- Simplicity is smarter than complexity.
- Doing nothing is sometimes the most powerful move.
- Money is a tool—not a trophy.
- I don't have to beat anyone. I just have to **stay aligned.**

What I Told Myself I'd Do in Tough Times

If you're reading this in a downturn, remember:

- Don't panic. You've seen red before.
- Check your thesis before your emotions.
- Losses aren't failures—they're feedback.
- Breathe. Revisit your journal. Stick to the plan.
- You didn't come this far to throw it all away over a headline.

What I Hope I've Learned by Now

I hope you've learned to:

- Respect the market—but not fear it.
- Read more companies than comments.
- Follow your system, not the crowd.
- Talk more about strategy than screenshots.
- Stay curious. Stay human. Stay grounded.

A Message from Me to You

[Write anything here. Freestyle. A message of hope. A mantra. A joke. A line you wish to remember. An apology. A note of pride.]

What Would Make Me Proud 5 Years From Now

Not the highest return. Not the fanciest holding. But this:
That you showed up. That you didn't quit. That you learned. That you still felt like **yourself** while growing.
With clarity, with care, Your past self—still learning, but already proud,
[Your Name]

Where to Store This Letter

- Digitally: Email it to yourself with the subject "Open on [5 Years from Today]"
- Physically: Print and tuck into your journal, portfolio binder, or under your favorite book
- Set a calendar reminder for 5 years from now: "Open your 5-year letter"

What This Letter Will Give You Later

- Perspective when you feel lost
- Encouragement when you feel small
- Clarity when you feel rushed
- A reminder: **You were always playing your game.**

Investor's Manifesto

A declaration of clarity, calm, and commitment.

I am not here to predict the market. I am here to understand myself within it.

I will not chase trends, tips, or headlines. I will chase discipline, awareness, and alignment.

I may not always buy at the bottom or sell at the top. But I will always buy with clarity, and sell with integrity.

I do not fear red screens or falling prices. Because I have chosen to play the long game—not the loud one.

I will not measure success by someone else's timeline. I will measure it by how well my money supports my mind, my values, and my life.

I believe in:

- Simplicity over sophistication
- Peace over performance
- Consistency over brilliance
- Time over timing

I will remember:

- That wealth without awareness is noise
- That every loss is a lesson
- That I am not my portfolio
- That the market is my mirror—not my master

I do not need to win every trade. I only need to stay in the game—without losing myself.

This is my manifesto. Not for perfect investing, but for purposeful living.

Further Reading

Books That Deepen the Game

Explore beyond the numbers—into mindset, meaning, and mastery.

This book was never just about stocks.

It was about becoming **a clear, calm, and conscious investor**—someone who grows not just wealth, but wisdom.

If *Game* helped you get started, these companion books will help you go deeper. Each one explores a specific dimension of investing, self-awareness, or decision-making—without complexity, fear, or fluff.

These aren't textbooks. They're **tools for reflection and evolution**.

Here are your next steps:

The Active Mind

How to think clearly in a noisy, uncertain world.

This book explores how thoughts become decisions—and how decisions become destiny. Especially relevant for investors who want to sharpen their mindset, avoid mental traps, and build inner clarity before touching their outer assets.

Read this when: You're stuck between "Should I act?" and "Should I wait?"

The Equation of Life

Where strategy meets soul, and success meets self-respect.
This book expands on the emotional and philosophical side of decision-making. It teaches how to align money with morality, goals with ground realities, and ambition with ethics.
Read this when: You want your wealth-building to feel more human—and less mechanical.

Live Fearless with Fear

Why fear never really goes away—and how to grow with it.
A vital read for investors who panic easily, struggle with risk, or feel overwhelmed by uncertainty. This book will help you redefine fear as a teacher, not a threat.
Read this when: You're scared of making the wrong financial move—or scared of making any move at all.

Manifestation: From Nothing to Everything

A bold, beautiful look at how intention shapes reality.
This isn't about manifestation in the pop-culture sense. It's about understanding how every outcome starts from awareness, clarity, and quiet action. A deeper, more spiritual companion to your investing journey.
Read this when: You're wondering how money, mindset, and meaning can all align.

Self-Help: New Syllabus

A realistic reset for those tired of toxic hustle and hollow advice.

If you've ever been overwhelmed by motivational books or disappointed by "success formulas," this book is your detox. Practical, honest, and refreshingly grounded—just like *Game*.
Read this when: You want to build a better life, not just a better portfolio.

The Human Game

A new perspective on how to play life with strategy, heart, and depth.
This upcoming book explores the inner psychology behind human behavior, choices, and consequences. It expands your view from market moves to life moves—and helps you play both with grace.
Read this when: You're ready to think beyond investing—and into legacy.

Where to Find These Books

All titles are available globally via:

- D2D (Draft2Digital)
- IngramSpark
- Kindle / Amazon
- Kobo, Apple Books, Google Books
- Zenodo (for open-access reflections and reports)

Or visit: https://www.sandeepjchavan.com/

Final Thought:

These books are not sequels. They are layers—each one bringing you closer to clarity. Because the true investor isn't just building wealth. They're building **awareness, alignment, and peace.**

Choose what calls to you next. And keep playing the game—**your way.**

Acknowledgments

Because no game is played alone.

This book was written with clarity—but it came from years of chaos, curiosity, trial, and quiet observation.

To every student, friend, reader, and investor who ever asked me, *"But how does the market really work?"*—this book is partly your voice. You didn't just inspire it; you shaped it.

To my family: thank you for giving me the space to think, teach, stumble, and return stronger. Your faith never came with conditions, and that's what made it unshakeable.

To the markets themselves—strange, humbling, poetic machines that reflect human behavior better than any mirror—I owe my deepest lessons. You don't reward brilliance. You reward presence.

To my silent mentors: Warren Buffett, Charlie Munger, Howard Marks, Naval Ravikant—and the countless unnamed thinkers whose restraint, rather than noise, influenced my own.

And finally, to the reader: Whether you picked this book up in fear or curiosity, seeking guidance or relief—thank you. You didn't need another finance manual. You needed a companion. And if I served that role, even briefly, I'm honored.

This book isn't the end of the conversation. It's the opening bell.

Let's keep playing.

— *Sandeep Chavan*

About the Author

Sandeep Chavan is an independent thinker, educator, and prolific author whose work bridges the gap between practical wisdom and profound insight. With over 100 published books across finance, philosophy, psychology, science, and personal development, his writing offers clarity without complexity—and depth without pretension.

As the founder of Gyrus Institute, he has mentored thousands of students, not just in academics, but in decision-making, discipline, and life strategy. He believes that investing is not merely about money—it's about **aligning wealth with awareness.**

Known for simplifying difficult ideas and rejecting the noise of popular trends, Sandeep continues to challenge conventional thinking on how we learn, live, and grow. *Game* is his attempt to bring peace and purpose to the world of investing—without turning it into a race or a roulette table.

When he's not teaching or writing, you'll find him observing people, deconstructing systems, or quietly choosing the simplest solution in the most complex situations.

Disclaimer

This book is intended for informational and educational purposes only. It is not, and should not be considered, financial, investment, legal, tax, or professional advice.

The views and strategies shared in this book are based on the author's personal experiences, research, and observations. They are not tailored to any specific individual's financial situation, risk tolerance, or goals. Readers are advised to do their own due diligence, consult certified financial advisors or investment professionals, and consider their unique circumstances before making any financial decisions.

While every effort has been made to ensure the accuracy of the content at the time of writing, the author and publisher make no representations or warranties of any kind, express or implied, about the completeness, reliability, suitability, or availability of any information, product, or service mentioned herein.

Investing in the stock market carries risks, including the potential loss of principal. Past performance is not indicative of future results.

By reading this book, you accept full responsibility for your own financial decisions and agree that the author and publisher are not liable for any outcomes resulting from the use of this material.

Did you love *Game: How to Play the Share Market*? Then you should read *India: The Investment Magnet*[1] by SANDEEP CHAVAN!

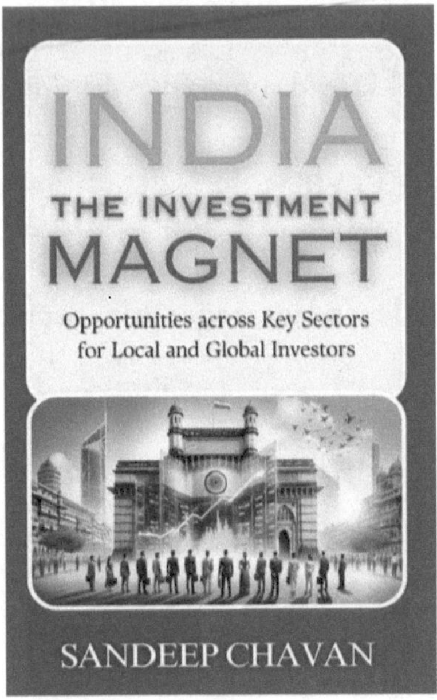

[2]

India: The Investment Magnet provides an in-depth exploration of the opportunities and challenges in one of the world's most dynamic and promising economies. Authored by **Sandeep Chavan**, this book serves as a comprehensive guide for investors, entrepreneurs, and leaders seeking to navigate and capitalize on India's transformative growth story.

The book highlights India's strengths as an investment destination, from its robust economic resilience and innovative

1. https://books2read.com/u/3GqOBP

2. https://books2read.com/u/3GqOBP

industries to its policy-driven growth and favorable demographics. It delves into key sectors shaping India's future, including information technology, renewable energy, healthcare, infrastructure, and agri-tech, providing actionable insights into their growth potential and investment opportunities.

Real-world success stories of companies like Reliance Jio, TCS, and Hyundai illustrate how businesses have thrived by adapting to India's unique market dynamics. The book also sheds light on the increasing role of retail participation, the evolution of India's stock market, and the emergence of midcap companies and government enterprises as attractive investment options.

With practical guidance on entering India's market, navigating regulatory frameworks, and forging successful partnerships, **India: The Investment Magnet** offers a roadmap for both seasoned and first-time investors. It emphasizes the importance of aligning long-term strategies with India's centenary vision for 2047—a future where the nation emerges as a global economic powerhouse.

Beyond numbers and data, this book captures the spirit of a nation that blends tradition with innovation, challenges with opportunities, and aspirations with action. Whether you're a global investor or a local entrepreneur, this book invites you to be part of India's remarkable journey—a journey of growth, innovation, and transformation that defines the 21st century.

Read more at https://www.sandeepjchavan.com/.

Also by Sandeep Chavan

Chavan's UED research

CMGED Research Report

Chavan's Cosmic Continuum (C^3)

Frequency

Ripples of Reality

Reality Realigned

The Great Realignment

I – The Cosmic Leverage

Chavan's Cosmic Theory of Relativity (CTR)

Chavan's Theory of Light

Echoes of War: The Russia-Ukraine Conflict and Its Global Ripples

Shattered Lives

The War Economy

Borders Redrawn

Arms and Allies

Collateral Damage

Justice in the Ashes

Somewhere in the Darkness of the Cosmos

The Blueprint of the Universe

The Cosmic Breath

The Eternal Sage Chronicles

The Sage and the Sovereign

The Family Pillar

The People's Flame

The Warrior's Soul

The Bridging Mentor

The Guiding Light

The Exodus

The Last Cycle: 2075

The Fundamental Theory of Life & Existence

Energy in Action: The Soul Demystified

The Active Mind

Energy in Connection

Death: The Disconnection

Subconsciousness: The Chosen Disconnection

Desires: The Engine of Life

The Restoration of Human Knowledge

Restoring Bhagavad Gita

The War of Thoughts

Cracks in the Known

The Human Game

The Divine Dilemma

The Original Intent

The Answers

Ultra Modern Life Philosophy

The Duality of Laughter and Tears

Take It Easy

Compare to Accept

Standalone

It's Not AI, It's AHI - Amplified Human Intelligence

The Decision Paradox

The Four Sapiens

Malicious Script of Indian Polity

The IIT Legacy & Global Impact

The IIT Legacy & Global Impact

You are just a Version of Your Original

Win the Game You Didn't Choose

Always Keep Your Bags Packed
Reveal to Shield - Learn the Game of Facades
Engage Beyond Elections
Culture, Identity & Change: The Evolution of Indian Society
The Triangular Dynamics
Never Trust Without Doubt
If You Can't Change the Country, Leave the Country
Live Fearless with Fear
India: The Investment Magnet
Realignment
Powering a Billion Dreams
Universal Skill
Extension: From Brush to Algorithm
Human Side of Einstein
The Future Knows No Lines
Let's Bring the Generations to the Table
Unified Energy Dynamics
A Beat That Never Dies
Strategic Horizons
Right From Scratch
The Forgotten Innovators
Physics Fixing
The Savior Illusion
The Selfish Side
The Age of the Weakest Sapiens
Neural Wars
The Absorption: There Is No Death
Strange Therapist
Bubbles: Become a Drop
Beyond the Blue
Half-Scholar

The Law of Truth

Failure

Philosophy 2.0: A Structural Manifesto

Chaos: A Gentle Guide to the Unresolvable

Self-Help: New Syllabus

Rippling

Game: How to Play the Share Market

Watch for more at https://www.sandeepjchavan.com/.

www.ingramcontent.com/pod-product-compliance
Lightning Source LLC
La Vergne TN
LVHW090320210926
848480LV00001B/311
* 9 7 9 8 2 3 1 7 0 4 8 1 1 *